PREACHING ABOUT DEATH

Eighteen sermons dealing with the experience
of death from the Christian perspective

edited by

Alton M. Motter

FORTRESS PRESS   Philadelphia

Library of Congress Catalog Card Number 74–26336

ISBN 0–8006–1098–9

4636J74   Printed in the United States of America   1–1098

CONTENTS

FOREWORD

This book is about death. It deals with those universal experiences related to the cessation of our human pilgrimage on the planet Earth.

All eighteen contributors write from a Christian perspective. Coming from ten Christian communions, including Protestant, Eastern Orthodox, and Roman Catholic, they form an ecumenical sample of today's Christian thinking and preaching on this subject. The fact that they come from fourteen different states adds to their representative character.

There is great help and guidance here for the reader who seeks additional insights about the experience of death. The writers speak from their hearts and minds as parish pastors, college and seminary professors, and bishops.

A few sermons are quite personal and strongly autobiographical. William Snyder's sermon on the death of his mother, and Homer McEwen's conversation with an Atlanta grave digger, come in this category, as do those of Keith Irwin and Carl Marbury.

Charles Harris, Harold Hatt, and Chester Pennington give valuable psychological insights about death.

Accepting death as part of a "cosmic cadence" is effectively portrayed by James Cox, Paul Davis, Daniel Durkin, and Howard Hageman. Death, as a part of God's will, is expressed in still different ways by William Buege and Michael Rogness.

Meeting death with faith and dignity is strongly emphasized by Gene Bartlett, Walter Burghardt, and Herman Stuempfle.

But the crowning theme which runs through nearly all of these meditations is the clear proclamation of Alexander Schmemann and Paul Washburn that "Christ is risen!".

And because he lives we too shall live!

August 1, 1974   Alton M. Motter

MEETING DEATH WITH DIGNITY

Gene E. Bartlett

Minister, The First Baptist Church in Newton
Newton Centre, Mass.

To us he always will be a young man because he never had a chance to be anything else. As a boy he had wandered into an urban church looking for recreation. What he really found was a life work. After college and seminary he was called back to the staff of that church to minister to youth even as he had been ministered unto. In due time he was called to the chaplaincy of a women's college. Shortly after he took up residence there with his wife and four children he learned the hard truth: death was near.

With great courage and sensitivity he recorded his thoughts in the days that followed. Included in that journal was an imaginative moment in which he wrote: "It's such a temptation. The phone lies here by my fingers on the bed. I've already called my doctors, my family and my friends, my lawyer and insurance man. They all know I'm dying, but what can they do? Their sorrow is comforting somehow but they're as helpless as I am. If only I can get through on the line to God. I could give him my reasons why I should be spared. Why did he have to do this to me? I'm only a young man with a promising future. True, those who are younger and more promising have died, but that's God's problem, not mine. I'm cultured, educated, a lover of the arts, a peaceful man. True, I've had more chance than those millions of hungry and deprived, but I've been on God's side, doing his work in the world. True, I have not done much for world peace or race relations, social justice, helping those in need, standing with those who suffer.

"Why is it always so hard to plead our vested interest before God?

"There lies the telephone. How many digits would we have to dial, do you suppose?"

1

One way or another, Glenn Brown must have found his way
through, for he faced death as he had met life, with dignity and
strength.

Not far from all of us is the hovering awareness that one day we
too will have to confront death, for those we love and ultimately
for ourselves. Where is an encompassing and enabling faith to be
found for an experience like that which is both the ultimate mystery and the ultimate reality?

A phrase in the classic eighth chapter of Romans has that rugged
simplicity which marked the Apostle Paul at his best. It is both a
personal confession and an affirmation of our shared faith: "I am
persuaded that neither death nor life can separate us from the love
of God which is in Christ Jesus our Lord." These are among the
most cherished words in the whole New Testament and there's a
reason for it: they are the Christian faith brought to simplicity and
maturity. They place life and death as two parts of the whole
human experience.

I

There have been generations in the Christian faith when we lost
that balance by saying: *death, not life.* There have been centuries
in which the Christian faith has been interpreted as preparation for
a life to come, not so much a fulfillment in life at present. Life was
interpreted in terms of death. Death was the first fact and life was
the derivative. Whole theologies and life styles have been based
upon that basic understanding. Life could be understood only in
terms of imminent death. So Thomas a Kempis whose "Imitation
of Christ" stands after five hundred years as one of the great works
of devotion, still could say about the teaching of Christ as he saw
it, "He teacheth them to despise things earthly and to love heavenly things; to neglect the world and to desire heaven all the day
and night." One of the Protestant preachers put it in another way
when Richard Baxter said that he always preached as a dying man
to dying men. So death was sovereign over life.

II

Partly it was in rebellion against this that our secular world has
reversed the formula. We are prone to say: *life, not death.* The

affirmation of the present world has set the tone for much of our secular life.

Perhaps a spokesman for that would be Henry Thoreau. When it seemed to his friends that death for him was near one of them, Parker Pilsbury, pressed the question of whether he had any vision of the other side. To this, Thoreau, practical even in the last moment of his life, replied, "One world at a time, Parker, one world at a time."

Less philosophical but more real to most of us are the practices about death which have become common, yes, even promoted. We do everything we can to make death look like life. We use the art of cosmetics to make the body look living. We avoid the hard but descriptive words. We make our burial places to look like parks, not cemeteries. But all this still seems to no avail for the matter is so much deeper than that. One of my friends who is a psychiatrist is persuaded that the real bedrock anxiety of human life, the source from which all others come, is the fear of death, recognized or unrecognized. So we affirm life to the denial of death with a kind of desperation, the anxious intensity born of the awareness that our denial really is not working at the deepest level.

III

It is against these distortions that the Christian faith emerges with such maturity as caught up in the letter to the Romans: "I am persuaded that neither life nor death can separate us from the love of God." That is a faith which lifts us into a total affirmation. It requires no denial, either of life or of death, because both are under God's sovereignty. As night and day are both part of any full day, so life and death are two sides of the whole human experience. Both must be included and seen as inseparable in our belief about life's meaning. It is not life as over against death, nor death as over against life, as though one were the enemy of the other. They both make up the human experience and must be understood together.

To be sure, we tend to begin our interpretation with life itself, and that is as it should be. If we affirm our hope about death, it is because life itself has given us due cause. One does not want or expect everlasting life who has not already received what Lowell called "intimations clear of wider scope" in his present experience.

So when Emerson wrote his famous line, "Whatever is excellent is permanent" it arose out of a deep personal experience, the death of his small son. In the light of that little boy's life Emerson could not conceive of its being temporary or passing. It was that same observation which prompted Professor Palmer to write a beautiful word about his wife, Alice Freeman Palmer, sometime distinguished President of Wellesley College. Professor Palmer said at her death, "One cannot view the facts of her life and not count the world irrational if out of deference to a few particles of disordered matter it should exclude so fair a spirit." So life gives us intimations about death and even times of illumination. It is persons we know and love who enable us to face the mystery of death with hope. Is life fashioned, often out of pain and anguish, only to be thrown away? The answer to that is not in logic, but in love. Life does instruct us about death.

But death also instructs us about life. Glenn Brown wrote honestly about that in his journal, in the last days of his life, "When the preciousness of life finally seizes you, that is the awareness that life really is sacred. . . . It is a great riddle to me as to why this should be revealed to the dying but hidden to those who are most involved in living." So the fullest meaning of life we can find comes from setting life and death side by side.

But the heart of the affirmation is that neither of these can separate us from the love of God. Both life and death are mysteries. In a sense we are living "after death" for the coming of life is at least as great a mystery as its continuance. After death is one mystery, but before birth is another! The only stability we know, it seems to me, is the belief that both mysteries are in God's hands. At last we are thrown back upon the simple but profound belief. Both life and death are in the hand of God and therefore will be used by the heart of God. Even in daily life we have to trust character when circumstances are baffling. We may say in a moment of uncertainty, "I don't know what this means at the moment, but I do know the person, and I trust him."

Some of the deepest beliefs we have about death are beyond proof, but not beyond what we would expect of God, as it has been given us to know him. When you say that death "cannot separate us from the love of God which is in Christ Jesus our Lord" you open the way to some great sustaining truths:

Because I believe in God I also believe there is some compensation in the whole cycle of life and death, some way in which those who have not been whole are made whole again, some way in which the stooped will walk tall, the limited will be liberated, the loveless will be loved, and the darkened minds will be illumined.

Because I believe in God I also believe that the hand which reached out to us in every other transition in life meets us in death too; that the voice which said when we moved from childhood to youth, from youth to maturity, and in times of crises, "Trust me and it will be well" will also be the voice on the other side of death's transition.

Because I believe in God I also believe that in some time, in some way, what is not known to us will be known.

Because I believe in God I also believe we can face death with dignity, not because we know what life to come will be, but because we know who will be there.

IV

The sum of it is from a story told in the terrible days of the blitz in London. It is said that a father, holding his small son by the hand, ran from a building which had been struck by a bomb. In the yard was a shell hole, and seeking shelter the father jumped in then held up his arms for his son to follow. But the small boy, hearing his father's voice urging him to jump, replied "I can't see you." The father, however, could see his son outlined against the night sky standing hesitant and anxious, and replied, "But I can see you. Jump!" So the faith that enables us to confront death with dignity is not that we can see, but that we are seen; not what we know, but that we are known; not that death denies life, nor life denies death, but that both are part of God's gift. Neither can separate us from his love. And that faith *does* give dimension and dignity to life.

IN THE NAME OF JESUS

William A. Buege

*Pastor, Lutheran Church of the Resurrection
St. Louis, Mo.*

There is a great deal that we can say about death because, if we have lived at all, we have not been unaffected by death. But whatever we might be able to say, it is at best a report or an evaluation of spectators. For all the tears that death has brought us to weep and for all the sorrows with which it has darkened our days and for all the threats with which it has constricted our hearts, we know death only from the rear, after it has passed by and left its unmistakable mark. Our knowledge of death is only secondhand, and that by itself should give us real pause. If death can do to us what it does only indirectly, then what will it do to us in direct personal confrontation?

It would appear that death not only marks the end-limit of our lives, but also the end-limit of what we can say. We still speak words about death, brave or despairful words, sympathetic or cold words, understanding or stupid words, but hardly meaningful words out of the understanding of personal experience and direct knowledge. We just don't know what it means to die and so we either try to live by ignoring death or we try to give explanations that really explain nothing except our own folly. We know beyond all doubt that we shall surely die, but we choose to live as though we shall never die.

Wittingly or unwittingly we erect our own little defenses against death to make life tolerable. The most simplistic defense is to regard death as natural, to hold that it is as much a part of life as breathing, even though it means that we breathe no more. We easily overlook the fact that death by its very nature is the contradiction of life, the total negation of everything involved in living.

It may be natural for plants and animals to die, but it is unnatural for man to die, unless human life is no different from animal and plant life. We may choose to look at death that way, but then we should note well that it is by our own free choice that we do so.

Free choice, however, means the exercise of our individuality which makes us persons. And that is the direct opposite of animal and plant life. In fact, death finally exposes the many false views of human life, life in the mass, life whose only goal and greatness are the state, life as a series of many or few cogs making up the machinery of humanity. When death finally comes, it comes as the ultimate contradiction of the impersonal because it comes to the individual who must meet it alone.

Death shows that man is person, however much he may have denied his personhood while he lived. By death man hears himself summoned, even though he never before acknowledged any summons from above or beyond or outside himself. Now man finally is addressed as "Thou" from a source which he cannot but obey and in a manner which gives him no choice except to respond with a very personal, "Here am I!" We may let others deceive us and we may deceive ourselves as long as we live and never ask, "Who am I?" But death unveils all little or big deceptions and convinces each with unanswerable finality that he is a responsible person, however irresponsibly he may have lived. Now at the last a response is wrung out of man if it is not willingly given. Now man learns to know himself as a person who is answerable, because he is compelled to say "yes" when death calls him and must go whither death beckons him.

And it is just this fact of our being persons who are responsible and answerable, that shrouds death in mystery and fills it with terror. What happens to this "I" that so boldly occupied the center of its universe and proclaimed itself its own god, at least its likeness to God, by insisting that it knew what was good and what was evil for it? What kind of a god am I, if I can determine everything else about myself, except that which in the last analysis determines me, and if what I hear at the burial of others is the ultimate truth about myself? "Dust thou art and unto dust shalt thou return!"

Death is the boundary which human pretensions cannot cross, the limiting condition which reveals human pride for the vanity that it is, the ultimate demonstration that while man is a person, even the lord over all creation and in a class by himself, he is still a man and not God, human and not divine, mortal and not eternal. Only a blind refusal to acknowledge our own death, even while we make every possible preparation for it by paying for what we ironically call "Life Insurance" and by purchasing a plot in a cemetery so that our dead bodies will one day have a place to be laid, can keep us dependent on ourselves alone and high in our regard for ourselves. Our successes are ephemeral at their best, and our fulfilled desires are no more than the lusts of our perishing flesh, and our vaunted independence is the braggart but tragic boast of life which is silenced once and for all by death.

But is that all we can say about death? Is it only the inescapable certainty that each one of us will one day hear himself designated with: "Thou shalt surely die!"? Is it all negative, consigning us to a pessimism that robs our little lives of any value and our present role of all purpose? Are we to live lives of bondage because all our days are passed in the fear of death? Is there nothing higher or better than the attitude which is best summed up with: "All right! If that's the way it is, then let us eat, drink, and be merry, for tomorrow we die!"? From a human point of view, that's pretty much all that is left to us as we rapidly move toward that evening in which our day is far spent and there is nothing ahead but the dark night which knows no morn.

For the person who still owns God as his God in any meaningfully personal way, the last word which he hears under the shadow of approaching death is: "Be not deceived! God is not mocked!" Death accuses us of having been self-deceived in our attempts to live apart from God and debase ourselves into something less than persons who always are such as they stand before God. We thought to mock God by acting as though He were not God and did not personally address us with, "Man, where are you?" As a result, death makes its rightful claim on us and parts the bushes behind which we sought to hide and exposes the nakedness of our shame which we sought to cover with our inadequate fig leaf.

Finally, death drives us out of the land which we so diligently cultivated as our personal paradise because we would not answer when God asked, "What is this that you have done?" We would not live as persons because we would not respond to God and so death puts an end to us as the persons we tried to be in dialogue with ourselves alone.

But isn't that even worse than anything else that might be said about death? However gloomy our human assessment of death and however final death's verdict upon what we know as life, it is as nothing compared to death as the judgment of God. Then it is not merely the end of what we make of life, but the total condemnation of what we have made of life. It is altogether irrelevant whether our varying views of death are worse or better, hopeless or hopeful, discouraging or encouraging. If at no other time while we lived, certainly in the face of death we will finally learn that whether we like it or not, truth alone is decisive. When death comes, there will be no time left for kidding ourselves and pampering ourselves and mollifying ourselves. Then all wishful thinking and every available kind of escapism will be left behind like frivolous companions who leave us in the lurch when we need them most, and we will have to go it on our own, naked and alone. We may have been drunk on the heady wine of life for life's sake and self for self's sake, but death ushers in the truth which sobers us from our binge and brings us face to face with the unanswerable, "Now what?"

And yet, death as God's judgment and God's condemnation, for all its severity, is the truth which alone gives us some knowledge of what lies hidden in mystery and the only real hope that can keep us from despair in our last hour. If death were merely natural or if death were nothing more than fate brooding over all that is human or if death were only the last test of man's stoic bravery, we could not tolerate it. It would deny our individuality and make nonsense out of all our ideals and reveal as folly what are our noblest aspirations. The glorious achievements of our science and the lovely harmonies of our music and the desperate striving of our most dedicated social endeavors, would be nothing more than the tale of an idiot, sound and fury signifying nothing.

But if we accept death as our just dessert from the mighty hand of God, then our death has something to do with the God who has something to do with us, and we are not orphans crying in the night of our aloneness as we crawl out of and back into a little

speck of dust way off in a forgotten corner of infinite space. Then
God is the living God who does not ignore us, even if his
acknowledgement of us is the sending of his last messenger, death.
As a bare minimum, communication between God and us is not
fully and finally broken off, if death is his spoken condemnation
upon us. The lines are still open, if for no other reason than to
speak his last word to us, "Return, ye children of men!"

But if that is a last word of God, there must be other prior
words of God to make this one his last word. If we can take,
indeed, must take, death from the hand of God, there is at least
something by which God reaches out to us. Then we can ask if
death is all that that hand has to offer. If through death God tells
us, "Return, ye children of men!" then we are not going into something that never ever was for us. We are going back where we
came from. Apart from God, death is a monstrous insult that we
cannot accept. Under God, death, even at its very worst, must serve
God's purpose and therefore cannot be a slide into the meaninglessness of nothingness.

When we receive death as from God, even his judgment as a
fitting end to what we have made of life, then our own personal
attitude toward death and the manner in which we see death, will
be altogether dependent on who our God is and how we hold he is
disposed toward us. If we know God as the source and ground of
all, then our death is our being returning to its source and ground.
If God is the grand all-soul, then death is our soul returning to
that wholeness of which it is only an infinitesmal part. If God is
the great ideal, then our death is whatever is ideal about us returning
to the fullness of the ideal of which we gave only the faintest
reflection.

The Christian faith holds that Jesus Christ is the way, the truth,
and the life by whom we can come to God as Father. That changes
nothing about death as verdict, nor the life-finalizing word to us,
nor God's mighty hand humbling us. But the purpose of God in
our death cannot negate his love in Christ and his mighty hand can
only be the hand of our Father.

And that changes everything. The inescapable summons,
"Return, ye children of men!" is the Father's call to come back
home where we belong, no longer to live like strangers in exile,

still less like prodigals wasting their substance in riotous living and ending up in a pigpen. In Christ God cannot be the destroyer of life. He is the creator of life who always creates out of nothing and therefore must first make nothings out of us in death in order to make something of us. Life even before death, has a different dimension than what is evident, because it is life with God as he offers to be God to us in Jesus Christ. And that's what faith in Jesus Christ is, life which is life in his name, life lived under the known love of God in Christ Jesus our Lord. And—that's the love from which nothing, not even death, can separate us, because herein is love, not that we loved God, but that God so loved us that he gave his only-begotten son for us.

So we believe and so our life becomes a following after, forgetting those things which are behind and looking forth unto those things which are before, in order to press toward the mark for the prize of our high calling of God in Christ Jesus. He died for us that we might live and he lives for us that we might never die.

"I DO": A CHRISTIAN APPROACH TO DEATH*

Walter J. Burghardt, S.J.

Professor of Historical Theology,
Catholic University of America
Washington, D.C.

Last year a respected medical doctor wrote in a respected medical journal: "In my opinion death is an insult; the stupidest, ugliest thing that can happen to a human being."

A startling sentence. The instinctive Christian reaction is to deny it outright. But the longer I look at it, the more tempered is my reaction. That sentence forces three profound questions: What does it mean for a human being to die? What did it mean for Christ to die? What should it mean for a Christian to die?

I

What does it mean for a human being to die? Two years ago a Catholic philosopher penned some profound reflections on the death of his wife. One passage is particularly pertinent: "A cow or a chicken is in some sense replaceable when it dies. But in the death of a person, there is a loss of something absolutely unique. When an animal dies, there is the loss of an 'it'; when a human being dies, an 'I' is lost to the world and a 'thou' to the survivors."

There, for me, lies death's "insult." A unique I, an irreplaceable thou, is destroyed. I who lift my eyes to the stars and only yesterday looked down on snow-capped Alps; I who catch with my ears the rapture of Beethoven's Mass in D and once throbbed to the music of my mother's voice; I who breathe the smog of New York,

* This sermon first appeared under the title, "The Life and Death Question" in the April 21, 1973 issue of *America*, © copyrighted by America Press, 1973. It is reprinted here under the above title with the permission of *America*.

12

whose nostrils twitch to the odor of Veal Scallopini; I who cradle the Christ on my tongue and gently caress the face of a friend; I whose mind ranges over centuries and continents, to share Plato's world of ideas and Gandhi's passion for peace; I who laugh and love, worry and weep, dance and dream, sing and sin, preach and pray: this I will be lost to the world, this thou lost to those who survive me.

This I God will not replace, cannot replace. I am not just *someone*; I am *this* one. For good or evil I touch a whole little world. And when I die, this warm, pulsating flame of human living and loving will die with me. Little wonder I don't care to die; little wonder I don't want to die.

II

What did it mean for Christ to die? Theologians are still groping to grasp it. For his death, too, was unique. The I that died on Calvary was not only an unrepeatable man; the I was God-man. It meant that he suffered not less but more; more exquisitely and more brutally, with an awareness, a sensitivity, that no other person could parallel, no mere man rival.

But why? Because with his death, death would cease to be "the enemy." Not that with Calvary death became easy; on Calvary Christ gave death fresh meaning. What that meaning is can be said quite simply and can be plumbed more profoundly.

Quite simply, from the death of Christ life was born. For us. God had decided that the oneness between man and God which had been ruptured in Paradise would be re-established on Calvary, that divine love would recapture man's heart through crucifixion —not the crucifixion of man, but the crucifixion of God! "When I am lifted up from the earth, I will draw all men to myself" (John 12:32). That is why, for me, the most rapturous words in the Gospel are the short words our Lord spoke to his apostles the night before he died: "I have life, and so you will have life" (John 14:19).

With these words we can plumb more profoundly the meaning of Calvary; for here, if anywhere, is the marrow of John's Gospel. It is Jesus who has life; Jesus *is* life (John 11:25). That is why the First Letter of John opens as it does, an ecstatic affirmation of him who is life: "That which was from the beginning, which we have heard, which we have seen with our eyes, which we have looked upon and touched with our hands . . . the word of life—the life was made manifest, and we saw it, and testify to it, and proclaim to you the eternal life which was with the Father and was made manifest to us" (1 John 1:1–2).

Jesus is life because the Holy Spirit, that Spirit who gives life, is his spirit; and this spirit, this life, this spirit of life, he gives to us. In John's vision, Jesus never really dies; for a man dies only if and when the spirit of life leaves him. That is why Jesus consoled a mourning Martha as he did. He was not satisfied with her belief in *another* life, her conviction that her dead brother Lazarus would "rise again in the resurrection at the last day" (John 11:24). No, "whoever lives and believes in me shall never die" (John 11:26). He is life, his life becomes our life, and that life need never leave us. That is why Jesus could say of himself: "This is the bread which comes down from heaven, that a man may eat of it and not die" (John 6:50).

In a word, the death of Christ is the death of death. "The ruler of this world is coming," he trumpeted at the Last Supper, "[but] he has no power over me" (John 14:30). At the very moment he "bowed his head and gave up his spirit" (John 19:30), he was gloriously alive, because the spirit of life was still and forever his spirit, his life.

III

What should it mean for a Christian to die? What it meant for Christ. Oh yes, an I is lost to the world and a thou to the survivors. That was true even of Christ. Death is indeed death.

But more importantly, death is life. Not only shall I not die altogether, totally, utterly; that is so frightfully negative. Death is that unique point between time and timelessness when the spirit of Christ, the spirit of life, can finally take complete possession of me, permanent possession, without my earthbound resistance. Death is that extraordinary experience when the Christ who *is* life fashions me finally to his life.

With St. Paul the Christian should be able to say: "For me, life is Christ, and [therefore] death is gain" (Phil. 1:21). But this conviction compels a new attitude. I dare not be "resigned" to death: that is insufficiently Christian; I am still looking on death as "the enemy." In contrast, Karl Rahner insists that death should be an act I personally perform, not an experience I endure. Death is a yes, an "I do." When Jesus cried with a loud voice "Father, into your hands I commit my spirit" (Luke 23:46), he was affirming life. And this is what a Christian proclaims with his last breath: "I have life." Only with this attitude can death be an act I personally perform. *I die.*

I am not asking anyone to be enthusiastic about death. Even the Son of God did not quite scale those heights. I suspect I shall never really want to die—not because my faith is infirm, rather because there is so much life, God's life, right here—in myself, in those I love. The authentic Christian tension is not between life and death, but between life and life.

It is not enthusiasm but readiness; not surrender but a love-laden yes. Not many years ago a sixteen-year-old girl lay dying in a Phoenix hospital. A dear friend was a Carmelite priest. The last time he saw her he must have looked dreadfully upset. As he tells it, "she looked up into my worried and harried face and said: 'Don't be afraid.' " Such, at its most profound, is the Christian theology of death: "Don't be afraid." It is most profound when a child can say it to an adult, a girl to a priest, when it is the dying who can say it to the living: "Don't be afraid."

"THAT GOOD NIGHT"

James W. Cox

*Associate Professor of Christian Preaching
Southern Baptist Theological Seminary
Louisville, Ky.*

The "text" of this sermon is to be found in both Scripture and tradition. That is, the background of all that I am going to say is the biblical revelation as a whole and what we know of the experience of the church.

William Manson used to say that the only God that the New Testament knows is the God of the resurrection.[1] We can go further and affirm that the only God that the Old Testament, as well as the New Testament, knows is the God of the resurrection. God stands over every experience of death, as life-giving power, able to breathe into the moribund culture, society, or individual and make it come to life.

Dylan Thomas, the Welsh poet who was preoccupied with death and who died much too soon, admonished us, "Do not go gentle into that good night."[2] For most of us the admonition is unnecessary. Our whole being cries out again and again against death. We do not want to die; we do not want those we love to die; we protest the end or failure of every good thing we know. But somewhere we may learn the secret of how to make a good death, how to say at one and the same time, "Let this cup pass from me," and, "Nevertheless not as I will, but as thou wilt" (Matt. 26:39). And we may be willing to give up our best-loved to God, knowing that we have not lost them forever.

1. William Manson, *The Way of the Cross* (London: Hodder and Stoughton, 1958), p. 10.
2. Daniel Jones, ed., *The Poems of Dylan Thomas* (New York: New Directions, 1971), p. 207.

16

> People who die
> are so terribly
> gone,
> except to those
> who see beyond sight
> and hear beyond hearing.[3]

What do the Biblical revelation and our own experience say to us about death?

I

To begin with, the experience of life and death (and we cannot isolate death from life) has meaning.

Now *what* this experience means is not obvious. When we look at a corpse, what do we see? A dead body, nothing else. We do not see an immortal soul; heaven's doors do not swing open for us to see what is there. When we are in the grip of grief, it is easy enough to take a purely scientific position and believe no more than we can prove. Ignore the flowers and forget the warm words of encouraging friends for a moment: what you see is grim indeed. Meaning is not obvious; absurdity holds sway.

However, the Christian faith asserts that in the cycle of birth and life and death, meaning is universal. Whatever happens adds up to something—somewhere, sometime. Not a sparrow falls to the ground without the permission of the heavenly Father. Not a seed dies in the soil without hope of survival in a new form of life. In fact, Jesus chose the grain of wheat for an analogy of the profound meaning of his death. The seed disappears, decays in the ground, and apparently loses whatever meaning it has had. But that is not the end of the story, for new life comes forth from the old. Apparent meaninglessness is transformed: what emerges is full of meaning.

We must go a step further: not only is meaning universal, it is also particular. As such, meaning is very special. Even without our conscious cooperation, God can, to be sure, bring meaning out of our experiences with life and death. But you and I can choose the way life and death will go for us. Meaning in this special sense is wrapped up in our choices; we don't stumble upon it.

3. Antonina Canzoneri, *The Commission*, April 1974, p. 32. Quoted by permission.

Viktor Frankl, the Viennese psychiatrist, told of an elderly physician who could not rise out of a depression into which he had fallen after the death of his wife. Frankl asked him what difference it would have made if he had died before his wife. "Oh, for her this would have been terrible; how she would have suffered!" Then Frankl showed him that by surviving his wife he was actually sparing her this suffering and, in fact, suffering for her.[4] A new sense of meaning—a personal decision of faith—was the healing insight.

Philosopher William James said, "If this life be not a real fight, in which something is eternally gained for the universe by success, it is no better than a game of private theatricals from which one may withdraw at will. But it *feels* like a real fight."[5] No wonder the Apostle Paul urged, "Fight the good fight of faith!" (1 Tim. 6:12). God is at work when we fight to do more than hold on; he is especially and miraculously active when we deliberately choose to live and to die in his will courageously and victoriously.

II

Now, if the experience of life and death has meaning, then the meaning of this experience is extended and enriched by its continuation. In other words, if this life as we know it is good, it is better if death is not the end of it.

Of course, not all people see something beyond death. A Chinese friend said that the teaching of his childhood religion compared death to the burning out of a candle: when the last bit of wax has been consumed by the flame, it is no more; so it is with a human life—after death it is no more.

However, most people hold to some form of life after death: belief in immortality is well-nigh universal. We see the crude reflections of that faith in the magnificent pyramids of Egypt, where provisions for a future life were made in terms of the needs and experiences of this life. We see them, also, in our own country

4. Viktor Frankl, *Man's Search for Meaning*, trans. Ilse Lasch (Boston: Beacon Press, 1962), pp. 114–115.

5. William James, *The Moral Equivalent of War and Other Essays* (New York: Harper and Row, 1971), p. 88f.

in the Indian burial grounds, where mementos of the hunt and war give mute witness to the expectation of a happy life to come. We find in the Bible perhaps more refined forms of this emerging hope of the human family, where King David, lamenting the death of his infant son, affirms, "I shall go to him, but he shall not return to me" (2 Sam. 12:23); where Jesus says, "In my Father's house are many mansions" (John 14:2) and "Today shalt thou be with me in Paradise" (Luke 23:43); where the Apostle Paul declares that when we are absent from the body we are "present with the Lord" (2 Cor. 5:8).

III

Now if life as we know it and live it here on earth is good, if it is better because it continues without end into the future, it will be best of all when God transforms it to make it fulfill his final purpose for it.

Of course, we can think of the life to come as very little different from our present life excepting certain annoyances and evils. That is understandable: it is hard to visualize anything outside of our own experience. Yet it would be very unfair and untrue to the fact and the possibilities of the life beyond to limit it to what you and I now know and feel and think. The Apostle Paul, considering the realities of a world not accessible to our normal means of perception, wrote,

> What no man ever saw or heard,
> What no man ever thought could happen,
> Is the very thing God prepared for
> those who love him. (1 Cor. 2:9, TEV)

The shape of the life to come is what God will make it, and that lies in the realm of mystery. Like a tourist going to Europe from the United States for the first time, we may have some notion of what awaits us in the new and strange experiences into which we are about to enter. But like an unborn child, we are totally ignorant of some aspects of the world into which we are about to be born. Of this we can be sure: life in the world beyond will be vastly different. Jesus said, "The men and women of this age marry, but the men and women who are worthy to be raised from death and live in the age to come do not marry. They are like angels and cannot die. They are the sons of God, because they have been raised from death" (Luke 20:34-36, TEV).

Furthermore, not only can we be sure that life in the world beyond will be vastly different, we can also be sure that God is in control, that God is Lord—first, last, and always! The God who created man from the dust of the earth, so that man became a living soul, can also out of the dust of our earthly existence create an eternal existence. "Thanks be to God who gives us the victory through our Lord Jesus Christ" (1 Cor. 15:57, TEV)! The risen Christ is "the guarantee that those who sleep in death will also be raised" (1 Cor. 15:20, TEV).

THE CRUCIAL ISSUE OF MANY MANSIONS

Paul Davis

*Minister, First Congregational Church of Webster Groves
St. Louis, Mo.*

Come as we are in worship, we are united by a variety of common denominators. A number of common factors make us one. We breathe, our diaphragms expanding and contracting, as we draw the breath of survival. Air supports us from the atmosphere as food provides nurture from the green flow of the earth. In our dependence on the physical environment, we are united.

Further, we are one in our need for love and our hunger for purpose to the end that life be meaningful. Without love we perish. Where purpose vanishes, we know the taste of gray ashes. We are a single family in the emotional and spiritual needs we house.

And there is death. We are creatures who die, all of us, each of us one by one. And we are conscious of death, our dying. All people die. We die. And we know it.

Much of the anxiety in our life is, at base, anxiety about dying. Pascal put the problem when he confessed fear at his finitude in the face of infinity which, as he wrote, "I do not know, and which does not know me." And so did John Donne reminding us how the bell's toll cannot be ignored or hidden from anonymously: "Send not to hear for whom the bell tolls. It tolls for thee."

Death is confronted, not ignored, in the heritage of the Bible. The psalmist intones the pathos of our situation, as people eventually swept away "like a dream, like grass . . . like a sigh." Again and again Jesus urges the disciples to face the approach of his death at Jerusalem even as he points to the resources of God within death and beyond it. Deep are the biblical resources for coping faithfully with death, in particular, with our individual dying.

The Bible helps us to meet death realistically. Jesus died. We die. And spiritual health is to face that reality, so the evasion of death need not hang like a shadow over our living. Death is not our deepest problem. More central is our fear of dying. Death, when faced, often loses its devastating power. Jesus at his final meal with his disciples carried immense authority. Part of his authoritative impact was in his talking so candidly with them about his approaching death. Some people I have known have taken the measure of death by learning to talk about their own death before its arrival. Help in meeting death realistically, not evading but facing, is one deep resource in the Bible.

Another is being as sure as we can about the quality of our living. The Gospel of John describes Jesus: "In him was life and the life was the light of men." Is our life profoundly lighted? How great is the quality? Are we so alive as to die the right death, not dying spiritually inch by inch and along the way somewhere? The real point is to be alive in a certain way. For once alive in a certain fashion, we discover it doesn't matter much what follows.

Still another biblical resource helps us in dying our death in a setting of stewardship. "Do not be anxious about your life," encouraged Christ as he held before us the images of birds in air, lilies in fields nurtured daily in the giftedness of God.

We who are anxious about our death can come to terms with the miracle of our birth. It is a miracle that we were born at all. To live any time at all is to be in the presence of miracle, life as a miracle of absolute caring. In spiritual terms it is what theology means by the word "grace," a beginning with gift and opening out, mounting up from there. It is the sense that if life can be this, there is no knowing what else life can be, life a landscape with a sign in front announcing "NO LIMITS." The image of life as gift animates the worldview of the Bible. To be stewards of our life, in its giftedness, its grace, provides resources of the first rank for dealing with the death issue.

But enough of generalization. Death comes in particular. We die specifically. What specific resources for death does the biblical life provide?

The 23rd Psalm offers two resources we explore now in particular, specifically, in greater focus.

The first, that death and dying involves what is involved in so much of life: the courage to adapt faithfully to change. Writes the psalmist: "The Lord is my shepherd . . . he makes me lie down in green pastures. He leads me beside still waters. . . . He leads me in the paths of righteousness. . . . Even though I walk through the valley of the shadow of death, I will fear no evil." To paraphrase that: dying happens in a context; at the time of death most people have traveled already a considerable distance; and the key to distance is also the key to death; the key is the courage to adapt faithfully to change.

Some of our most basic anxieties stem from this: we are creatures of habit and we love routine; yet life, by its nature, is always changing. And how we respond to anxiety stirred by change affects profoundly the shape and the length of our days.

Living is a matter of life and death. Most people who come to death have lived and died and lived again many times. In the pilgrimage of growing up, the infant must die for the child to live. The child dies to make way for the teen-ager. The teen-ager dies so the adult may emerge. And so into old age, a living and dying forward, life into death, death into life.

It is the same with social roles we fill. Single man to husband, childless couple to parents, parents to grandparenthood, a series of births and deaths mark our way, opening our way to life.

Biblically the theme of change suggests rich resources as we deal with death. For in the biblical experience, it is transition which provides the scene of God's self-disclosure. Early the exodus, later the national trauma of exile, still later Christ whose power reveals itself through suffering: the biblical pattern of God amid change, the holy in the mobile again and again present themselves.

God accompanies us in change. Through transition he abides and leads on as our companion. On this the Bible speaks clearly and with power. And so in our dying. God, who companioned our birth, moves alongside each turn in our pilgrimage and remains friend and lord in our death. God, present to all prior transitions, is present to death. His power, in all moments prevailing, in the hour of our death goes forth.

The first resource then, the first in the psalm, the 23rd, is courage to adapt faithfully to change.

The second resource is awareness of death as enlargement, a change opening on expanded peace, a deeper freedom. "Though I walk through the valley of death, I fear no evil . . . Thou preparest a table before me . . . I shall dwell in the house of the Lord for ever."

People limit themselves more than they need to limit themselves, more than was intended. One such restriction is in thinking of human life too entirely in terms of body. Another is in conceiving the universe a provincial road instead of a broadly promising highway.

First, body: when illness invades the house of our body, sometimes our response is anger at the body, fury in feeling the body has let us down and betrayed us. I sat once with a man, hospitalized, in the final stages of cancer. He was in anguish at what the illness was doing to his body. Reaching for some way to help him find spiritual power, I finally said intensely: "Look, you and I are not much longer interested in your body. God is not interested in your body; God is interested in *you*!"

Body does not identify human beings. Body is not irrelevant to human beings. But we are more than body. We are body plus. Learning to see our body for what it is frees us to image more fully our wholeness. As long as our imagination remains trapped at the level of body, we do not see the fullness. The Apostle Paul saw it: "In earthen vessels," he said—body as vehicle, he meant. Would that the excellency, the power, the glory, be of God, the ultimate Father: how it finally is, what and whom it finally is about.

Dying suggests the picture of old shoes, having traveled, now worn out. We put them aside, with some sadness, for we have been fond of them. But we are not angry at the shoes. They have served their purpose. In similar fashion, an aging car, a dress outdated, a worn suit are put aside. There comes the time of separation, and we part. But we discard rather than reject.

So with death. We are not contained between skull and feet. We are not imprisoned inside nerve pulsations, flow of blood, and heartbeat. So the body dies? So? We have this treasure. The things which are seen are temporal. The things which are not seen are more than that.

Thus body.

Then universe: more than provincial road, the universe stretches broadly as promising highway.

The best answer to skepticism is skepticism. Question: "Can you prove there is life after death?" Answer: "Can you prove there isn't?" To believe is to close the door on no possibilities.

On a night a few years ago, we sat with our childern, in the grass, all of us pondering stars and planets, galaxies of galaxies. And the talk turned to satellites and space travel and future promises. "Do people live on other stars and planets?" someone asked. To the same question put fifteen years before that, I would have answered some variation of, "Not that we know of" or "I doubt it" or "Definitely not." But when asked that night in the grass, I answered more simply: "They just may."

Thus the mood of the world more nearly matured, shocked out of older complacencies: "They just may." All kinds of things once thought impossible are now seen as possible. People broaden their horizons. Fewer are willing to say what can't occur.

In such a climate faith prospers, faith faithful in the face of dying. For if God be for us, who can be against any prospect, the higher side of any promise?

I shall dwell in the house forever, sang the psalmist. Jesus paraphased it, one great house, many rooms. "If it were not so, I would have told you."

It is important how Jesus put that. He would have told us of limited prospects, were they limited. But he left them open. He declared them open.

And so our clue.

"TO KEEP DEATH DAILY BEFORE ONE'S EYES"

Daniel Durken, O.S.B.

Associate Professor of Theology
St. John's Abbey and St. John's University
Collegeville, Minn.

Fourteen centuries ago the citizens of church and state had no access to morning newspaper reports of highway fatalities and the victims of Belfast bombings. They saw no nightly, 10 P.M. scenes of slaughter on the battlefields of Viet Nam, Cambodia, and the Golan Heights. They read no magazine accounts that recapitulated the week's grisliest crime spree. Lacking these day by day reminders from media so filled with dead-lines, a sixth-century religious leader, Benedict of Nursia, felt it necessary to include the following salutary reminder in his Rule: "To keep death daily before one's eyes".

To twentieth-century Christians that line may sound like a carry-coals-to-Newcastle recommendation. Our age is surely no stranger to the death that is kept daily before our eyes on the living room television set. We no longer need to prime our memory or imagination to make death come alive. Death indeed comes to us in living color between commercials that convince us life is just one pill, spray, ointment, capsule, tube, or can after another. Count, if you can, the number of killings, murders, and assorted deeds of deadly violence during an evening of television watching, and it becomes obvious that society is taking quite seriously that sixth century suggestion of Benedict "to keep death daily before one's eyes."

Yet death, for all its familiarity to our times, is still a foreigner who comes to many of us like the unexpected thief breaking into our home (Matt. 24:43). The death we see mass produced is death out there, across an ocean, across a continent, or at least

26

across town. As long as death can be kept on that twenty-one inch screen across the room we feel safe enough to treat death as just one more commercial—a household commodity readily available to everyone, but we have no big wish or rush to buy it now.

But a funeral puts death into sharper focus. A funeral translates the daily death of Benedict's reminder into the context of a certain day, today. A funeral is the time and place to respond to that call of the Scriptures: "Exhort one another every day, as long as it is called 'today' . . . For we share in Christ, if only we hold our first confidence firm to the end, while it is said, 'Today, when you hear his voice, do not harden your hearts . . .' " (Heb. 3:13–15).

Today's funeral is that call of Jesus Christ to all of us not to harden our hearts, not to become callous or forgetful, not to ignore the advice "to keep death daily before one's eyes." We who pray, "Give us this day our *daily* bread" (Matt. 6:1), we who praise, "Blessed be the Lord, who *daily* bears us up" (Ps. 68:19), we are the same ones to whom it has also been said, "If any man would come after me, let him deny himself and take up his cross *daily* and follow me" (Luke 9:23).

This daily remembrance of death is no morbid fear of dying that paralyzes activity and makes us fretful. To be mindful every day of our mortality is to be aware of that natural process which is as obvious and inevitable as the setting of the sun. We can keep death daily before our eyes because each day dies before our eyes, each day turns gray and a little colder, every day repeats that essential cycle of life and death. Indeed, "this is the day which the Lord has made" (Ps. 118:24), for it is a day never again to be repeated. There is only one May 1, 1974 in all the world and in all its history. And yet this unique, unrepeatable and irreplaceable day must come to an end, it must leave its appointed time and place to make room for tomorrow. What a jumble we would have if each day declared its inalienable right to hold fast and firm and not be moved.

Our life is like our day, for we, too, die a little day by day. We give of our time and talent, of our love and care, of our work and worry, and these we cannot reclaim or recall. We can neither stop the world to get off nor reset the clock. Kodak to the contrary, no moment can really be captured. Time is too free to be shackled. As

God's free children, we likewise move as time marches on, and there can be no clinging or grasping to childish wishes or adolescent ways. We must let go as surely as dawn lets go of day and day lets go of twilight.

To doubt death daily or to deny death daily is therefore tantamount to insisting that our individually charted orbit of life has ended the age-old search for perpetual motion. To keep death daily before one's eyes is to be attuned to the world's rhythm and to be sensitive to the cosmic cadence. When we say with the pride of St. Paul, "I die every day" (1 Cor. 15:31), then we have heard the music of the stars, the song of the world, the melody of mankind, and the tune of our own life. Then we are ready not only to die daily but also to sing, to dance and to live daily.

To be caught up into the rhythm of life and death that each day measures out for us is to have firm hope in life after death. The psalmist says it so simply and clearly when he prays,

> I wait for Yahweh, my soul waits for him,
>   I rely on his promise,
>   my soul relies on the Lord
>   more than a watchman on the coming of dawn.
> Let Israel rely on Yahweh
>   as much as the watchman on the dawn! (Ps. 130:5–6)

Has any watchman ever been disappointed in the return of another day? Surely not. Just as night must always give way to light, so also must death always give way to life. Jesus who is the light of the world has assured us that "whoever believes in me may not remain in darkness" (John 12:46). Each day grows dark so that it may play the surprise of growing light again. We live in order to die, and we die in order to live. This rhythm of humanity is as basic and pronounced as the rhythm of a Viennese waltz. This rhythm keeps us moving, singing, dancing and living through the darkness of death "until the day dawns and the morning star rises in our hearts" (2 Peter 1:19).

This funeral, this day of death, this today when we have no choice but to keep death before our eyes is also a celebration and a day of life. Every day will bring closer the fulfillment of that promise made to us in the spirit by Zechariah when he assured every generation of believers and lovers that "through the tender mercy of our God, the day shall dawn upon us from on high to give light to those who sit in darkness and in the shadow of death, to guide our feet into the way of peace" (Luke 1:78–79).

Every day that looks at death with the eyes of faith will look beyond death to see the vision of the new heaven and the new earth and the new city that John describes in his Revelation: "The city has no need of sun or moon to shine upon it, for the glory of God is its light . . . And night shall be no more; they need no light of lamp or sun, for the Lord God will be their light, and they shall reign forever and ever" (Rev. 21:22; 22:5).

LIFE AND DEATH

Howard G. Hageman

President, New Brunswick Theological Seminary
New Brunswick, N.J.

Two books stand next to each other on one of my library shelves. One is Jeremy Taylor's classic, *Holy Dying*, a manual from the seventeenth century indicating what Christian behavior should be during those last hours. The other is a strange little volume published in Cologne in 1557 entitled *Imagines Mortis*. At the top of each page is an appropriate verse from scripture such as "O wretched man, who shall deliver me from the body of this death?" or "Sitting in darkness and the shadow of death," while beneath the verse is an illustrative woodcut, almost always containing skeletons, the figure of the grim reaper, or men and women whose faces are contorted by terror.

We all know that for centuries this morbid fascination with the art of dying was a stock item in Christian piety. Both Christian art and Christian poetry are filled with it. We also know that in recent days there has been a strong reaction against death, a reaction so strong that death has been sentimentalized almost out of existence. "He is not dead; he is just away." "The rose has grown over the wall." These are typical expressions of the way we tried to hide the fact of death, much in the same way that the carpet of artificial grass is used to conceal the grave in the cemetery.

It is perhaps unfortunate that now the curve seems to be swinging us to the other way, back to a fascination with death and dying which, however useful it may be psychologically, is still unsatisfactory from a biblical or a theological point of view. The great thing about the Bible is that it in no way seeks to minimize or to conceal the fact of death. It is there from the very beginning, there, as a celebrated British theologian once remarked, as the "sacrament of sin." Nothing that the Bible says from beginning to end in any way alters that fact.

But because of the event of the death and resurrection of Jesus Christ, there is a whole new way of interpreting that fact, not the sentimental way of artificial grass and paper flowers, but the gospel way of responsible obedience.

We do not have to read very far in the New Testament before we begin to realize that if we want to talk about death we must start by talking about life. This is Paul's point in Romans and it is a point made over and over again. For the man who has lived his life purely in terms of self-seeking and self-satisfaction, death is one thing, and a pretty terrible thing at that, while for the man who has lived his life in responsible obedience to his Lord and to his brother man, death is something entirely different. To pirate a favorite phrase from the Middle Ages, the "art of dying" depends largely on the art of living. *If we live, it is for the Lord that we live, and if we die, it is for the Lord that we die.* (Rom. 14:8)

That may sound like sentimentalism, but it is not; it is an attitude which is based squarely on the cross of Jesus Christ our Lord. So long as we persist in seeing that cross as a piece of theological algebra or as the tragic martyrdom of the good, we are not likely to understand what Paul is getting at. We have to see it for what it was, the most profound statement in history of the meaning of life and death. For paradoxical as it may sound, from the Christian point of view real dying always involves living and real living always involves dying. Let me try to explain.

The gospel is full of exhortations that we must take up our cross and deny ourselves in the daily business of our human existence. This means saying "no" to ourselves, sometimes at trivial levels, sometimes at significant ones, but always learning how to think and act in response to something other than the inclination of our own egos.

But each one of those nos, each one of those acts of denial, is a little death, a partial destruction of the self that is in us all and controls us all. Presumably that is why more than one classic theologian has pointed out that the passion of our Lord involved far more than his hours on the cross. Literally it involved his whole life, for he was always being confronted by the alternative of accepting his own welfare or submitting to what he believed to be the will of his Father. Painful and dramatic as it was, the cross was simply the dramatic summary of what had been Jesus' whole life-style.

To accept his way of life, therefore, is to begin to die. Paul's statement was that he died daily, and that was no exaggeration. Never a day comes but that we are confronted, whether we are teen-agers or senior citizens, with the choice between living for ourselves or living responsibly, and every choice for responsibility is a further dying of the self. *If we live, it is for the Lord that we live.*

Now all that has to be said before it is possible to say anything about the Christian attitude toward dying. If that attitude is not linked in the closest way to the Christian attitude toward living, it is hard to know what can be said about it that is not either terrifying or shallow or sentimental. Living depends upon dying and dying upon living. James Martineau, the philosopher and theologian of nineteenth century England, wrote these words when he was ninety and asked to put something in a child's autograph book:

> To a child new born, Life has for a few years all the joy of a playground and a holiday, and Death, when he hears of it, the terror of a spectre in the dark. To the Christian re-born, it is more awful to live than to die, seeing that he may live all wrong, but cannot die amiss; for the one, managed by his own weak hands, may at any moment become guilty; the other, determined by the wisest will, cannot fail of being best.

But then, what about dying? If living means living for the Lord, how can dying mean dying for the Lord? We can see it easily enough in the case of those who give up their life for the faith, in the case of a Paul, a Polycarp, a John Huss, a Dietrich Bonhoeffer, but how can it apply in the case of American church members like us who will probably die in a hospital bed with IV needles in our veins and an oxygen tent as our final home? How do people like us die for the Lord?

Well, for one thing it needs to be pointed out again that giving up our lives for the gospel is not confined to a one-time act of martyrdom any more than the passion of Jesus Christ was confined to the cross. If we have been living for the Lord, that kind of responsible obedience has been part of our daily experience. Even while we have been living we have been dying for the Lord. *If we die, it is for the Lord that we die.*

But now, how about the reverse? Is there any sense of the word in which it can be said that, even as we have been dying, we have been living? Seen from a New Testament point of view, the answer has to be "yes." For the New Testament always sees a double meaning in the two words, "life" and "death". Death is the act of physical dissolution which marks the end, but death is also the denial of the ego, the destruction of the self. And life is the business of existence, breathing, eating, sleeping, but life is also the profoundly satisfying experience of living in obedience and responsibility.

So while any secular man of sense would say that we live to die, the Christian knows that we die to live; we keep denying the self and refusing the ego so that we may grow in our enjoyment of real living, abundant living, or, if you like, eternal life. It is the death of our selves that releases us into this new way of life, into new patterns of existence, into the new creation which came with the resurrection of Jesus Christ from the dead. This is why John always speaks about eternal life not in a future, but in a present tense. This is why Paul writes about displaying both the death and the life of Jesus in his own person.

For the act of dying when it happens has now become only the dramatic symbol of what has been happening all along, the passage through death to life. All of the little dyings to old habits and the little resurrections to new ways of being that have marked every day on our calendar are now gathered together into one frightening but significant symbol, the symbol of dying to the Lord as we have been doing all the days of our life.

Nor is such a faith mere speculation. It accepts the fact of Easter as the central fact of the Christian gospel; it takes seriously the claim that he who died to life on the cross is indeed the pioneer, the first to experience the full reality. "Death is swallowed up; victory is won." The last enemy has been destroyed, destroyed in the moment that the passage from death to life was finally and fully made on Easter morning.

I am the first to admit that such a faith leaves many questions, troublesome questions, unanswered. It gives us no clue, for example, to the question why we die so differently, and at such different times. Nor does it give any satisfying descriptions of what that new life is like. All kinds of people have tried to fill in the gaps with all kinds of answers, most of them pretty empty and shabby. The time schedule (as if that made any difference to one who inhabits eternity!) has never been published and the sequence of events is a problem that can be debated from now till next Fourth of July without ever reaching an answer.

All such things may appear to be troublesome when the Christian claim about death and life is examined from the outside. It is only those who are on the inside who recognize its essential irrelevance. If that seems like an elitist remark, it is! It obviously requires a certain kind of life-style before dying can be put in any new perspective. And that is nothing strange; every human relationship has its full depths of meaning only for those who are personally involved in it. "How can she possibly love him?" we ask about a marriage which strikes us as highly unlikely, yet the marriage is working and working well. "I don't understand how they can be such good friends". But they are.

"Such a way of looking at death and dying looks incurably romantic to me." I am sure it must, but come and try this way of living for a while, try it seriously, and then let's hear what you have to say. For if a man lives to the Lord, does it seriously and with purpose, it is bound to have a deep effect on the way he looks at death. For death is never a problem to be solved in isolation, but an inevitable part of the whole human story. And if we say we are the servants of Him who has transformed the whole human story, then how can we possibly not believe that death and dying have been included in that transformation just as much as life and living? *If we live, it is for the Lord that we live, and if we die, it is for the Lord that we die.*

VICTORY OVER DEATH

Charles U. Harris

Dean Emeritus, Seabury Western Theological Seminary
Flint Hill Farm, Delaplane, Va.

Father Andrew Greeley of the National Catholic Opinion and Research Center was quoted in the national press recently as saying that there are four great basic issues of our day: how to secure order and justice; how to resolve the conflict between good and evil; how to relate the sexual revolution to the Christian faith; and how to deal with the question of life after death.

It is this latter question which draws our attention today. It is not an easy question to deal with nor a popular one. In a small dynamic country church, the death of a young woman member prompted the minister to prepare a series of thoughtful sermons on death. But the obvious discomfort and anxiety that the sermons produced caused him to terminate the series prematurely. Death is not a question we like to face, as so many of us know when our lawyers suggest that we draw or up-date our wills.

Yet it is a question that lurks always in the background. "In the midst of life, we are in death." It must be dealt with and it is better to do it in the context of normal life than to be compelled to do it in the context of bereavement when we are often unprepared to do so.

What is death? Despite the necessary attention given this question in the Journal of the American Medical Association and the press, death can be defined in simple terms. It is the termination of physical existence, nothing more, nothing less.

The old truism that there are only two certain things in life, death and taxation, is, for the Christian, only half true. The termination of physical existence is not the termination of life. Death for us is a "rite of passage" to use Margaret Mead's term. While it

is manifestly true, and undeniable that our existence in physical
form ends, it is also equally true that we do not cease to exist.
Instead, we move from one state of being to another state of being.

When I was a child in confirmation class, a time when street cars
were a familiar sight on the city streets, the minister likened death
to changing street cars, as we did when we transferred from one
car to another to reach our destination. It was a simplistic explanation, perhaps, but descriptively adequate for a child's mind.

But almost anything else we might say about death would be a
generalization and to be viewed with suspicion. To have meaning
death must be considered in the concrete situation. Death is a very
different thing to you if you are the person who is dying; or if it is
your father or mother; or your son or daughter; or a casual
acquaintance; or three hundred people killed in the crash of an air-
plane in a foreign country, none of whom you know.

But three things are common to most of us. Each one of us must
make the final "rite of passage." Each one of us has, or must have
at some time, to face the death of a loved person. And we must all
face the painful, overwhelming, sometimes devastating fact of loss
in every death which has reality for us.

Loss is the way death is experienced, loss for the person who
dies and loss for those who loved him or her. The loss is real. It is
undeniable. It is a fact we cannot run away from or hide from. Not
all the Bible texts or polite, compassionate euphemisms in the
world can take away its hurt. If they could, then the love which
bound the living and the dead would have been unreal and had no
meaning. But it is real and has meaning.

One of the comforting discoveries of our time, a discovery
which thoughtful people have always known, is that loss is best
assuaged by grief. That may sound foreign to a person brought up
in a society which admires the stiff upper lip, the tearless eye, the
business-as-usual approach to loss. But as wise men have always
known, grief is not a bad thing to be repressed or held back or
hidden deep within ourselves. At least one great religious tradition
prescribes for its followers a specified time for mourning, a time
when the work of grief is to be done.

It is a necessary work, a time when it is good to shed tears, to
live with the hurt and melancholy of the soul, to think and speak

of the beloved departed, of the times of joy past, of days of laughter and sunshine, of battles fought together, of suffering experienced together, of all the moments which united two lives as one.

The work of grief is made easier for us when it is met with the loving, quiet, compassionate support of our family and friends. Most comforting of all is the presence in prayers and sacrament of Christ, a presence which seems to break through all mundane concerns to comfort and to assure and to encourage in times of grief.

So is the work of grief done until we are able slowly to rejoin the living in the concerns of the living, remembering with the most constant affection the departed, but having assimilated into our experience their loss creatively and constructively as the Lord would have us do.

But how will you or I respond to the news of our own impending death? W. C. Fields, the famous comedian of another era lay dying in a hospital. He was not known to have any religious affiliation or sentiments. When his friend and drinking companion, John Barrymore, equally famous as an actor, came to see Fields in the hospital, he found him reading the Bible. Barrymore expressed surprise. In explanation, Fields said to his old friend, "When the fellow in the yellow night shirt comes, I want all my bets covered."

Only a vivid imagination would characterize death as "the fellow in a yellow nightshirt." But when we learn that he is not far from us, we may, as my aged mother did, welcome him as a friend, as the relief from pain and suffering. Or we may respond in fear and dread.

On the purely human level, research at the University of Chicago's Billings Hospital has shown a pattern of reaction which to many people provides a source of solace and which may help us face the end. When the approach of death is sensed or learnt, the first reaction is to deny it, to say, it can't happen to me. Then as its certainty becomes more apparent, resentment and anger follow as one wrestles with the question, why me? Then, at last, comes an acceptance of the fact and a withdrawal, slow but actual, as one anticipates the loss of loved one, home, friends, possessions, and life itself until, at the end, fear has vanished and, in many ways, the world has been shut out. The great Pope John the twen-

ty-third, on his deathbed, wearied by the attentions of well-mean-
ing people, said, "Please let me be. A Pope must die with dignity." And a friend, a doctor who spent his internship and resi-
dency at New York's great Bellevue Hospital, said that in all his
experience there he had seen only one person die with a fear of
death and he was a young person with an incurable disease.

This sermon is cast against the backdrop of the Christian religion. One summation of its teaching about death is found in the
Easter Communion Preface of the Book of Common Prayer which
tells us that Christ "was offered up for us and hath taken away the
sin of the world; who by his death hath destroyed death, and by
his rising to life again hath restored to us everlasting life."

Christ's resurrection from the dead has destroyed the power of
death and has given back to us our ancient birthright, everlasting
life. On one occasion he said, "I am come that they may have life
and have it more abundantly." His meaning was clear. Life is not,
as the pagans believed, a gift bestowed at birth and relinquished
when their span of earthly life was ended. Life continues after the
physical dissolution of the body. The ego, the person signified
when you say "I", the thinking, willing, remembering self, continues to exist with such opportunities of fuller growth and life as lie
beyond the powers of imagination.

Paul wrote in his first letter to the Corinthians, "Now if this is
what we proclaim, that Christ was raised from the dead, how can
some of you say there is no resurrection of the dead? . . . If Christ
was not raised, then our gospel is null and void, and so is your
faith." He then adds this clinching argument, "If it is for this life
only that Christ has given us hope, we of all men are most to be
pitied." But Christ has abolished death and the "dead shall rise
immortal." "Death is swallowed up," he cries out, "victory is
won." (1 Cor. 15:12–58).

Thus in the greatest and most solemn moment of life, the
moment when the fellow in the yellow nightshirt reaches out for
us, when earth's small victories pass away, when the pain of loss
becomes unbearable and the fear of the unknown blackens the
mind with anxiety, when the body's pain becomes more than drugs
can contain, and loneliness and physical decay intolerable, when
the lightning shaft of personal disaster takes away the beloved

youth in his prime or the revered citizen, let us look once again to the roots of our Christian belief. Here we find the incomparable assurance of a love that will not let us go, in the person whose earthly life in the flesh was poured out on Calvary's cross and who was given life again by the Father. In the victory of his dying and in his resurrection, we share. This is our hope and surety. This love will never let us go, in this life or in the life to come. So with the pilgrim folk of all the ages we proclaim with confident faith, "Thanks be to God for the victory which overcometh death."

THE PERPETUAL FINALITY

Harold E. Hatt

Professor of Theology and Philosophy, The Graduate Seminary
Phillips University, Enid, Okla.

A young couple were travelling with their child to visit Grandma. The child began talking about the things he would do with Grandpa during the visit. Since Grandpa had recently died, the young couple exchanged glances by means of which they decided to say nothing. However, when the conversation did not switch to another topic, but became even more animated, another exchange of glances brought them to the decision that it was time to say something. In as calm and reassuring a tone as possible, the mother said to her son: "That won't be possible, Tommy. You know, Grandpa died." The child's response, mingling just a touch of disgust with profound exasperation, was: "What! Again?"

I suppose the finality of death is far from self-evident. In children's play, somebody who is dead does not stay dead. It is even possible to be dead, but not to lie down. The one who is on the receiving end of "bang, bang you're dead" does live to play another day.

But, if you will excuse the paradoxical phrase, in real-life death there is an inescapable finality. In the succinct and sombre statement of Scripture: "It is appointed unto men once to die" (Heb. 9:27a, KJV)—"It is appointed for men to die once" (Heb. 9:27a, RSV). In death there are no second takes, no second chances. To be sure death is a complex process, rather than a simple event. Some people may find themselves in the very jaws of death and live to tell about it. But once we die, there is no one who can live to tell about that. Death is an inescapable finality.

However, my text is not the biblical statement about death as our inescapable fate. My text is rather taken from a chapter in which

Paul's Gospel is expressed in terms of the significance of the resurrection of Christ Jesus. In this context we find a statement about the human situation: "I die daily" (1 Cor. 15:31b, KJV)—"I die every day" (1 Cor. 15:31b, RSV). Although equally succinct as the passage of Scripture referred to earlier, this statement is not equally sombre. The overtones here are not those of future judgment but of present triumph.

It is the work of Christ that transforms us from victims of death to victors over death. However, this transformation, both for Christ and for us, is not a movement away from death but through it.

Christian faith offers us no escape from the finality of death. What it does do is to open up the possibility of a transformation of death from the inescapable finality to the perpetual finality. The death that comes but once is transformed by being set within the experienced of the death that comes daily.

What is the underlying strategy or dynamics of this transformation? Is the daily death a kind of innoculation, so that small doses of death initiate a resistance against feeling its full force? Is this a specific example in which we apply to death the general principle: "If you can't lick them, join them"? What goes on that has the power to transform death from an inescapable finality to a perpetual finality? If the finality of death remains, where is the basis for a sense of triumph?

Taken by itself, the statement that "I die daily" could be as much an assertion of defeat as of confidence. As Shakespeare's Julius Caesar reminds us, cowards die many times while brave men die but once (*Julius Caesar*, II. ii. 32–37). And yet, Paul's assertion that he dies daily is not cowardly flight from impending death. It is a courageous facing of death like that portrayed by another of Shakespeare's characters, Duncan's queen in *Macbeth*. She is described as "oftener upon her knees than on her feet." Perhaps in allusion to our text, it is said of this saintly lady that she "died every day she liv'd" (*Macbeth*, IV, iii, 110–111). Apparently she shared with Paul the courageous credo which proclaims the faith: "I believe in life, and in death as a part of life."

What is the difference between the daily dying that is a cowardly defeat and the daily dying that is a courageous triumph? In the former, we are overwhelmed by our sense of the transitoriness

and contingency of life. In the latter, we have achieved a conquest
of the transitoriness and contingency of life. The Christian response
to death is more than merely becoming aware of its inevitability.
We are summoned not merely to await death but to consent to death
in the conviction that grows from faith in the power of Jesus
Christ's death and resurrection.

There is a danger in all talk about "consenting to death." Such
concern with death can be morbid or it can be wholesome and
healthy. Attending to death can be life-denying or life-affirming.
Awareness of death can dull or sharpen our awareness of life. If
such ambiguity is possible, is it not more promising to try to ignore
death and go on about our business with the life that is at hand?
The fallacy in this line of reasoning is that ignoring death can be
as ambiguous as concerning ourselves with it. To ignore death can
be a realistic appraisal of the difference between what is and what
is not within our control, or it can be a reaction of terror in the
face of that which is beyond our control. The person who ignores
death has not necessarily shifted his attention to something else.
He may have a preoccupation with death that compels him to
drive it from his consciousness.

Is it possible to do more than to analyze the ambiguity of our
situation with regard to death? Can we find some positive guidance
directing us to the achievement of the positive potential and away
from the negative? Here we need to expand the focus from our
text to its context. When Paul affirms that he dies daily he does so
in the course of affirming his confidence in the power and significance of the death and resurrection of Christ Jesus. That is what
makes the difference between good news and bad news.

It is intriguing to me that it is the power of another event that
happened once for all that brings us out on the positive side.
"Intriguing" may not be an appropriate word here, for it is the
very heart of the gospel of which we are now speaking. It is the
unique event of Christ's death and resurrection that is proclaimed
as the power through which dying daily becomes an affirmation of
life. Because Jesus Christ died once, our dying once is transformed
by our dying daily. It is the power of the resurrection that gives us
life in the midst of death.

The resurrection is a source of both hope and judgment. Proclamation of the gospel of the death and resurrection of Jesus Christ means for us a word of assurance, and a word of demand. It evokes trust and obedience.

I have the hope that enables me to consent to die daily because Jesus Christ died once. Death is transformed from an inevitable finality to a perpetual finality through the power of the death and resurrection, and this is our hope. Death is the most forceful opponent, since it threatens us all with extinction and meaninglessness. But through the death and resurrection of Christ Jesus even this enemy has been defeated. A few verses preceding our text, we read:

> For as in Adam all die, so also in Christ shall all be made alive. But each in his own order: Christ the first fruits, then at his coming those who belong to Christ. Then comes the end, when he delivers the kingdom to God the Father after destroying every rule and every authority and power. For he must reign until he has put all his enemies under his feet. The last enemy to be destroyed is death (1 Cor. 15:22–26, RSV).

A few verses following our text we read:

> When the perishable puts on the imperishable, and the mortal puts on immortality, then shall come to pass the saying that is written:
>
> > "Death is swallowed up in victory."
> > "O death, where is thy victory?
> > O death, where is thy sting?"
>
> The sting of death is sin, and the power of sin is the law. But thanks be to God, who gives us the victory through our Lord Jesus Christ (1 Cor. 15:54–57, RSV).

But Christian faith does more than call us into a community of those who hope that the awesome power of death has been conquered. We die daily because we are called into a fellowship of suffering and service. Our faith in the redeemer who died for us on the cross prompts us to bear our own cross. Paul precedes and follows the statement that forms the text of this message with a rhetorical question:

> Why am I in peril every hour? I protest, brethren, by my pride in you which I have in Christ Jesus our Lord, I die every day! What do I gain if, human speaking, I fought with beasts at Ephesus? If the

dead are not raised, "Let us eat and drink, for tomorrow we die." Do not be deceived: "Bad company ruins good morals." Come to your right mind, and sin no more" (1 Cor. 15:30–34a, RSV).

I am not at all sure that the hedonistic philosophy which is referred to here is the best style of life even if death is the end of everything for us, even if it is the inevitable finality rather than the perpetual finality. And I am not sure that Paul means to imply that. What he speaks of here is the power of Jesus Christ's death and resurrection not only to free us from the power of death, but to fill us with a new power for life. Instead of clinging on to life, Paul was able to risk his life in order to accomplish something with it. We may not face the risks that he faced, but we can live life with the same determination to spend our lives for what we believe. To die daily, so that the inevitable finality of death becomes a perpetual finality, is to live a life of perpetual service.

To die daily is to live in newness of life. May the Lord who makes all things new grant us a new power to consent to death daily and to live each day fully. By dying daily we live most fully.

ON BEING CONSECRATED

Keith W. Irwin

Professor of Philosophy and Chairman, Collegium of Letters Eckerd College, St. Petersburg, Fla.

The Christian faith and the Christian life are grounded on the fact of Incarnation, Emmanuel, God with us in the person of Jesus of Nazareth. Death is a fact, inextricably tied to our bodily existence, as to that of Jesus. It is this child, that woman, this man who dies. The observance of death, even in a funeral or memorial meditation cannot be separated from the concrete reality of the person who died, lest, like those who have wished to separate the saving work of God from anything tainted by the concrete, material existence of Jesus, we run into the most blasphemous heresy. Therefore, no Christian funeral meditation can occur without that concrete reference. Though judgment, like grace, is dispensed by God, not by man, the minister cannot escape his call to serve God's ministry of judgment as faithfully as he does God's ministry of grace. The thin line, the narrow tightrope between hypocrisy and self-righteousness is the domain of the pastor's funeral walk. To keep faith with this definition of the territory of the funeral meditation I wish to present here just one of the many types of difficulty presented by the need for honest Christian reflection about human life. We never get to bury angels, and only very rarely saints.

"Thine, O Lord, is the greatness, and the power, and the victory, and the majesty: for all that is in the heaven and the earth is thine; thine is the kingdom, O Lord, and thou art exalted as head above all."

Dear friends, we are brought together on this afternoon, in this Christian church, by those most elemental forces that touch human life. Though we are many, and come from many places and walks of life, we assemble here, some willingly out of love, some uncomfortably out of duty, some fretfully out of an awareness of our common mortality, because a man's life has touched our lives deeply, and because he suffered, died, and left us. We come to commemorate, pay profound respect to, and mourn this man, George Adam Henley, for he was a good husband, a good father, a good friend, a good neighbor, a man as upright in character as he was in bearing and posture.

George Henley was born just over eighty years ago on March 30, 1893, the son of William and Elizabeth Henley, in the neighboring state of Kansas. He grew up on a farm, wooed and married his own Elizabeth, and they established a home as tenant farmers near the family homestead. After two sons were born to them, they moved here to Brownsville, and George became a rural mail carrier in the days before the automobile greatly simplified the rural mail carrier's job. A daughter came into their family, the years passed, George and Elizabeth reached the stage of no longer being considered newcomers to our community, and they began to be appreciated for the qualities of their family, the character of their children, Elizabeth's dedicated service to this church, George's vigorous participation in the affairs of our city. This appreciation has deepened steadily through the years until this hour when we come here with the members of his immediate family, his younger brother, Frederick, nieces and nephews, grandchildren and great grandchildren, a great number of friends and neighbors, to celebrate George's accomplishments, to give thanks that we shared his life, and to search out its continued meaning for us.

How weigh a life? How reckon up on the balances the worth of any man? Who can judge in such terms that he is not judged in turn? Who sees the value of any man's life in the sight of God save God alone, and he sorrows and rejoices with all of us, and yearns for our good with a compassion that no mother-love or father-love can approach. It is to that yearning on God's part that we must address our attention, for the profit George's life holds for us, this gathering of people, containing in it Christians and non-Christians alike.

For one thing we cannot blink, in fairness to the integrity that marked George Henley's life. He did not consider himself a Christian. He was not ignorant of those professions that mark off the serious Christian's life, as they marked and indelibly stamped the life of the wife he dearly loved. His wife, some of his children, many a minister before me, friends from the church dearly desired and sought that this man with whom they shared so much might share with them what they understood to be the blessings of the Christian life. But George could never make Christian professions half-heartedly, insincerely, or just to please others, and by his own repeated assertion he never found, despite an openness to it, the evidences, the experiences, the convictions of heart and mind that would enable him to feel called to the Christian faith.

This pastor will take second place only to the members of George Henley's family in acknowledging the depth of a sense of ambiguity, of mystery, of poignant sorrow, as, utilizing those supporting words of Christian faith and promise in this service, we ponder their application. At no time does human love cry out to divine love from the depths of anxiety and hope more than at this time. How far does the writ of God's promise run? How broad a terrain does the domain of Christ's sacrifice encompass?

George Henley, in right mind and full possession of his senses, would have denied he was a Christian, but before any of us jump to the thought of this as a reproach, let us ask ourselves if any of us can equal his record of "doing good unto others." Christ died to save sinners. In our moralistic equations of sin, many of us, including this pastor, need Christ's death more than George did. Our Master admonishes all of us that concern for others is a more serious and significant indication of devotion to God than creedal affirmations and scriptural correctness without such accompanying service. "Not all those who say to me, 'Lord, Lord,' . . . but those who do . . . ." "Inasmuch as you have done it unto one of the least of these my brothers, you have done it unto me."

We can recount with warmth and appreciation the qualities of friendship, humor, genuine interest in others which produced a thousand—yes, a thousand—cards and letters of condolence and friendship in the month following his recent very serious surgery. The beautification of Main Street, the lighted field for recreation and sportsmanship, the hospital fund drive, the campaign to have our local river a part of the scenic river preservation act, the patriotic service of country, his friends who are here at this service from every segment of the population in this region, bespeak a contribution, made with no request or expectation of return, of the highest order of Christian brotherhood. Favored by a career in this community that took him out on the roads early in the morning, and brought him back to town early in the afternoons, George not only faithfully pursued that career for over thirty years, but used those afternoon hours up and down our town's by-ways doing good, and doing good with a quality and of a quantity that shames all those called do-gooders.

We need to remember as well the courage to accept declining health and the impairment of his physical vigor and activity. His unremitting cheerfulness, his eye to those whose sufferings exceeded his, was and is a testimony to the enduring resources of the human spirit to rise above the most crippling limitations. He never cursed life. He never cursed his illness. He did not curse the death he knew to be around the corner, but looked toward it with a quizzical cheerfulness.

If I were to exclaim, out of the admiration I feel for George Henley, "What a man!", I'm sure that, like a liturgical refrain, I would hear from this congregation an amplified echo coming back, "What a man!"

So we return to our question: "What value, what meaning, the Christian affirmation that George could never find it in him to make?" The doctrinal purist might fault me for dodging an issue, but I find a scriptural basis for a word of significant support and hope to many of us. In an either caricatured or neglected passage, the Apostle Paul talks about the sacramental character of marriage, and writing to Corinthian Christians with many concerns about the Christian ethic of love and marriage, Paul speaks once on behalf of the Lord, and once on his own behalf, in 1 Corinthians, the seventh chapter. On behalf of the Lord, for Paul finds it in Jesus's teaching, he says the wife should not separate from her husband, and that the husband should not divorce his wife. On his own behalf, for Paul finds no counterpart to this problem in Jesus's teaching, he says "the unbelieving husband is consecrated through his wife, and the unbelieving wife is consecrated through her husband." If Paul's concern for the questioning in his parish, and his compassion for them runs this deep, how can this pastor do less than emulate Paul? For in George and Elizabeth Henley's marriage of over fifty years those qualities of life whereby two people were of one flesh were extraordinarily present: Elizabeth, a pillar of this

Church, because of George's recognition of the profound support her faith gave her life and their marriage; George, a pillar of this community, albeit always without benefit of election or appointment, because of Elizabeth's recognition of the profound support his concern for others gave his life and their marriage. "If any woman has a husband who is an unbeliever, and he consents to live with her, she should not divorce him. For the unbelieving husband is consecrated through his wife . . ." (1 Corinthians 7:13, 14)).

The Christian affirmation *does* have meaning. And thanks be to God, through his servant Paul, that the deepest questionings of the hearts of George Henley's loved ones, find the answer that, in their love, they must have seen was there. Those fruits of love, as tangible as their offspring, are there for George and Elizabeth. Each has received richly from the love of the other, and the power of a Christian's consecrated life reaches out to those who have become of the one flesh of love, to a husband and on down to children.

George Adam Henley, a man consecrated by the good works of his life which will live on and speak of him long after he has left our physical presence. George Adam Henley, a man consecrated by the debt all of us gathered here gladly acknowledge we hold to him, a debt he was never concerned to record or collect on. George Adam Henley, a man consecrated by over fifty years of the reciprocally devoted love of a Christian woman. The poet has said that "death is musical in another melody." Other poets and theologians have talked about the mysterious ways of God. We rejoice today that one corner of that mystery has been lifted for us.

"None of us lives to himself, and none of us dies to himself. If we live, we live to the Lord, and if we die, we die to the Lord; so then, whether we live or whether we die, we are the Lord's. For to this end Christ died and lived again, that he might be Lord both of the dead and of the living." Amen.

ON WHETHER WE LIVE OR DIE:
FROM A BLACK THEOLOGICAL PERSPECTIVE

Carl H. Marbury

Associate Professor, New Testament Interpretation
Garrett-Evangelical Theological Seminary
Evanston, Ill.

The attempt to get at the meaning of life must inevitably face the question of death. This is so, if for no other reason than that death appears in each and every life. There is nothing more certain in life than death. It qualifies every moment of this advance toward death that we call life.

The fact that "none of us will get out of this life alive" is a sobering thought to contemplate. All living things die sooner or later, but of all living beings, man is the only one fully and frightfully cognizant of his imminent end. Unlike other living creatures, man has a distinct and clear sense of the possibility of nonbeing, that is, a time when he will cease to exist as a living entity of consciousness. Such a knowledge of nonexistence or nonbeing often heightens and exacerbates man's sense of anxiety and despair, so much so that it often becomes impossible for him to *live*. This is especially true of those who prefer to think that death is always someone else's problem and is no concern of theirs. Death is more problematical for us when we try to ignore it. We overcome the fear of it by facing up to it in the reality of what it is and what it is not. It is, indeed, for a Christian, an end, but not the end.

Death is inevitable. It is an enigma. It is a mystery, but then, so is life itself. The mystery of life and death persists despite man's unceasing efforts to unlock their mysteries—through story and song, through philosophical speculation and scientific investigation; through artistic expression and religious supplication. The human spirit has been, is, and will always be deeply involved in the relentless cycle of the mysteries of living and dying, of being and nonbeing, of existence and nonexistence.

Death is seldom as disconcerting and penetrating as it is when one faces the death of a "fellow creature" and in particular, of a person whom one loves and reveres deeply. Paul L. Landsbert[1] put it most correctly when he said:

> "The consciousness of the necessity of death is awakened only through participation, only through the personal love by which this experience is completely imbued. We have constituted an "us" with the dying person. And it is in this "us", this new and utterly personal being that we are led toward the living awareness of our own having to die . . . My community with that person seems to be broken off; but this community in some degree was *I myself, I feel death in the heart of my own existence*."

The most profound mystery of death surfaces therefore, in man's personal anxiety about death. The existential mystery is the fact that, *I, too*, must die—*I*, in my quality as a creature of consciousness, as a person of humanness, as a living entity laden with unique value, existing just once as the only exemplar of my kind, must be brought to an end. A dear one's death reminds me that I too have an appointment with death. It is for this reason that the words of John Donne ring true when he says:

> "Any man's death diminishes me, because I am involved in mankind."

Death means that one ceases to be, that here is a loss of identity as one becomes nothing—that is, "ashes to ashes and dust to dust." Paul Tillich said that one can be overcome with a sense of anxiety in the face of nonbeing because the finite self is threatened by nothingness on the one hand and meaninglessness on the other.

In Christian theology, death is ultimately a question of eschatology. This eschatology is filled with deep historical significance and spiritual meaning. When I was growing up in Alabama, my church had a senior choir which sang many Negro spirituals and "eschatological type" hymns whose lyrics spoke of death in some

---

1. Paul L. Landsbert, *L'Expérience de la Mort* (Paris: Declee de Brouwer, 1933), p. 18.

way. The same was true of the choirs throughout the rural areas of
the South. There are those who criticize the music, the preaching,
and the worship of these churches, accusing them of engaging in
"pie-in-the-sky", contemplation of the otherworldly and "escapist
dreaming" about going to heaven when there is so much to be
done down here in this world.

Some of these criticisms are no doubt justified, but basically they
are unfounded. The "spirituals" were not escapist songs of a
defeated and maligned people. The old "revival gems" were not
paeans of day dreaming and wishful thinking. They were and are
profound expressions of faith—about life and about death. When
Black people sang the old songs, they implied that death is not
really a future reality; it is a part of their everyday existence. Singing about death and about "life on the other side" is a wholistic
affirmation about a life firmly grounded in a God who is Lord of
both the living and the dead. By singing "eschatological" hymns
one is reminded of the words of Paul when he said:

> Death is swallowed up in victory.
> O death, where is thy victory?
> O death, where is thy sting? (1 Cor. 15.55)

Death is not a victory of tragedy but a celebration of freedom—
for those who live and die in the Lord. One is reminded of the
words of Dr. Martin Luther King's last sermon in Memphis, Ten-
nessee:

> "I *would like* to live a long life, but I have been to the mountain top
> and I have seen the promised land."

The epitaph of his tombstone reads:

> "Free at last, Free at last.
> Thank God Almighty, I am free at last."

Of all the people in this country, death is probably the least problematical to Black people and their cousins, the American Indians.
Death was often a constant companion and friend, because there
were some things worse than death:

> Oh Freedom! Oh Freedom!
> Oh Freedom, I love thee!
> And before I'll be a slave,

> I'll be buried in my grave,
> And go home to my Lord and be free.

The Black man has lived with death for all his sojourn in this country. His life was cheap if he showed any interest in freedom, and slavery was a type of death, that is, a living death more inimical than life itself. The slaves was an "it," an object, a commodity, a "nonperson." He was constantly harassed with the realistic threat of physical death, of which the dreadful overseer was the symbol. The slave had "no rights" which a white man was bound to respect since he was not a citizen said the judge in the famous Dred Scott decision. The slave was not a "happy" slave as some historians would have us believe. No slave enjoyed being "property" with no humanity and no human rights. No slave took comfort in his non-personhood. No slave rejoiced in the fact that he was a means toward an end rather than an end in itself.

This dehumanizing institution and the depersonalizing legacy of segregation, discrimination, and bigotry still operative among us, have wreaked psychological havoc and death on generations of human beings. Black people's attitude toward death has been profoundly influenced by this experience of life. Blacks tend not to fear death. Indeed, they fear life which has been far more miserable and agonizing than death could ever be. And so, they sang and still sing of death, not in some morbid sense, but in a profoundly victorious and eschatological manner. In singing about death, they made life livable. In other words they took the "sting" out of life. This attitude is very evident in Robert S. Arnold's old hymn, *No Tears in Heaven*:

> No tears in heaven, no sorrows given,
> All will be glory in that land; . . .
> There'll be no sadness, all will be gladness,
> When we shall join that happy band . . .
>
> No tears, no tears, no tears up there,
> Sorrow and pain will all have flown.
> No tears, no tears, no tears up there,
> No tears in heaven will be known.

We see it also in A. S. Bland's old hymn, *How Beautiful Heaven Must Be*:

We read of a place that's called heaven,
It's made for the pure and the free.
These truths in God's word He has given,
How beautiful heaven must be.

How beautiful heaven must be,
Sweet home of the happy and the free,
Fair haven of rest for the weary.
How beautiful heaven must be.

The creators of the spirituals expressed the same kind of auda-
cious faith affirmation about death. The spirituals express a festive
celebration of triumph over the ancient enemy of man. Howard
Thurman once wrote:

> The great idea in the *Spirituals* is that death itself is not *the* master
> *of life*. It may be inevitable, yes, gruesome, perhaps, releasing, yes;
> but triumphant, *Never*. With such an affirmation ringing in their
> ears, it becomes possible for them, slaves though they were, *to stand*
> anything life could bring against them.[2]

The spirituals are not poetic utterances of a defeated, naive
and other-wordly generation hoping to escape responsibility for
this life. They express an acceptance of one's fate but not of one's
conditions. We know this because of the many slave insurrections
which took place before the Civil War began. Life and death were
looked upon as one pilgrimage by the creators of these songs. It
was a pilgrimage of continuity, which transcended the fact of
death in a dynamic process moving towards fulfillment in the
knowledge of the Lord. There would be a time say the writers
when "the knowledge of God would cover the earth as the waters
cover the sea." The rhetoric of the spiritual, was deeply rooted in
the New Testament interpretation of the meaning of life-death:

Done made my vow to the Lord,
And I never will turn back,
I will go, I shall go,
To see what the end will be.
My strength, Good Lord, is almost gone
I will go, I shall go,
To see what the end will be.

2. Howard Thurman, "The Negro Spiritual Speaks of Life and Death," *The
Divinity School Bulletin*, vol. 45, April 16, 1948.

But you have told me to press on
I will go, I shall go,
To see what the end will be.

These songs of deep pathos and ethos are theological interpretations of life and death. They express, in symbolic terms, the profound conviction that God, the Lord of the judgment, was not done with his people—that God was not done with life. Death in the hands of God was nothing but "icing on the cake."

As Dr. Thurman says:

The consciousness that God had not exhausted *His* resources, or better still that the vicissitudes of life could not exhaust God's resources, did not ever leave them. This is the secret of their ascendancy over circumstances and the basis of their assurance concerning life and death. The awareness of the presence of a God who was personal, intimate, and active, was the central fact of life and around it all the details of life and destiny were integrated.[3]

Jeremy Taylor wrote:

"He who would die well must always look for death, every day knocking on the gates of the grave; and then the gates of the grave can never prevail against him to do him mischief."[4]

This sounds like another pious and naive statement about death, but much truth is contained therein. Like the old Black eschatological hymns and spirituals, Taylor affirms that we can come to terms with dying and death only if we understand it sufficiently so that we overcome our fear of it.

When one sees the meaning of life one is able to see the meaning of death. One cannot see the meaning of life apart from death or death apart from life. Black people have long taken the position that if you can't lick it—then join it, since God, through the death of Jesus Christ, has indeed taken "the sting out of death" just as he "takes" the sting out of life. The "sting" of death is depression, is despair, is hopelessness, is anxiety, making it impossible to live and to live more abundantly. For he who believes that Jesus Christ was indeed, "the resurrection and the life" affirms unequivocally in a faith that will not shrink.

3. Ibid. p. 17.
4. Jeremy Taylor, *The Rule and Exercise of Holy Dying* (Cleveland: World, 1952) p. 52.

CONVERSATIONS WITH A GRAVE DIGGER

Homer Clyde McEwen, Sr.

Pastor, First Congregational Church, UCC Atlanta, Ga.

Despite all the significant technological advances by which the race has invaded the shallow segments of outer space *man* is still *man's* most frequent subject. Numerous phases of prehistory and history have been sifted again and again as we strive to fathom the mysteries of our genesis and our evolution. Through all of this we have looked avidly for any signs which these investigations might give us apropos our final destiny. Much of this probing can be attributed to our intense, perennial desire to know self and universe; but lurking constantly below the surface is man's perennial lust to be as God is. An examination of the cyclic theological fads that recur from century to century, masquerading as novelties, reveals that when man feels himself to be the ascendant lord of creation his religious culture degenerates into ethical, gnostic, and humanistic postures for which God has little relevance.

But out on the darker layers of our mortality death persistently labors, methodically peeling away generation after generation, leaving each individual, however lowly or exalted, mute and cold, making no response to the circumstances of pomp or poverty surrounding the bit of clay. Many meaningful clues as to the paraphernalia which man brings to the crisis of bereavement can be discerned in the rituals and offices which accompany the ordeals of death, mourning, and adjustment. Though the means of disposing of the body may range from medical use for organ transplants to interment or cremation, the monolithic certainty of each individual's inevitable demise dwarfs and mocks all of man's fierce desires to continue in the flesh. Though the end is sure the superficial, regional funeral practices are noteworthy.

In New Orleans, Louisiana amenities surrounding bereavement include a "wake" where food and drink are served, attracting, among others, groups of free-loaders who are strangers to the deceased and the mourners. Interment is usually above or on ground level because sub-surface water would quickly fill graves dug into the earth.

In Brownsville, a slum community in Brooklyn, New York, the clergyman pronounces the words of committal in the church or chapel and does not accompany the family to the gravesite where the body is quickly covered by an attendant using a small bull-dozer.

On moving to Atlanta, Georgia, I discovered various funeral practices that were interpreted for me by the senior grave digger at the Southview Cemetery. He was a squat, powerful old man with a sense of command which reminded one that he had fought through the Spanish-American War as a staff sergeant. One quickly noticed that things usually went well when he was in the quartet of diggers handling the burial.

When my first Atlanta funeral brought me into his presence, he approached the group where I stood waiting for the pall bearers to bring the casket to the grave. Singling me out, he said, "You must be a new preacher around here. These Atlanta preachers don't come to the cemetery 'less it's a big shot or somebody what left them some money."

I smiled at him and replied, "Since everybody gets just as dead as the next fellow I come with every bereaved family. Why should we desert the mourners at the time of burial?"

"Well," he retorted, "I don't see what good all this does nohow. Men like you keep comin' out here talkin' about 'a sure and certain hope of resurrection through Jesus Christ.' Everyone of 'em is gonna die. And preacher there will be a hole for you, either here or some place else."

"Yes," I admitted. "But when that time comes God will have another minister standing at my graveside repeating that same hope and promise over me. And so it will be as long as the race survives."

For a moment he fell silent. Then, with a strange smile lighting his countenance, he said, "Now that's somethin' for me to ponder.

Never thought of it like that before. But preacher, dead is dead! Besides, you ain't talkin' about nuthin' you can prove."

And so it is that Christians pronouncing the hope of immortality over their dead speak of nothing which they can prove. For faith does not live within the narrow limits of what man can prove, but rather in the limitless realm of that for which he hopes. But so provident and merciful is our God that he gives us, even as we live in the flesh, experiences that foreshadow the complete life in him for which men hunger: Beauty which moves us to amazement and praise; truth which rebukes and cleanses the finite, fragmented knowledge which we laboriously acquire; compassion which chastens the feral yearning for power and self-assertion which may lurk at the center of every ego; and that ineffable thirst for the presence of the eternal which defies words and bursts the bonds of mere language, forcing us to resort to the symbolic music of poetry.

Christians need to acknowledge that our faith is not the only answer to the terrible question of mortality. There is the bottle into which millions of Americans crawl for temporary solace. There are the many drugs, both legal and illegal, which may temporarily dull our spirits to the galling anxieties of existence. But far deadlier than attempts at chemical cures is the deliberate decision to live without hope, accepting death as the dead end of all that is really human. Such a decision is a protracted spiritual suicide which one embraces while breath and pulse remain. Our hope in Christ outweighs and justifies every struggle, every doubt, every despair which moves us to accept with joy God's promise through our Lord, Jesus Christ, that man can emerge victorious over death. Moreover I am strengthened and encouraged by the power and beauty exemplified in the lives of men and women who live their days guided by the beautiful beacon of the immortal hope. As they live with faith in the promises of Christ their lines of march along this pilgrimage become trails of light that we follow with joyful confidence. For they go not as miscreants to a deserved doom, but rather as forgiven servants of God, approaching the time and place where the redeemed of the Lord shall see him darkly, as through the glass of our fleshliness, but face to face.

The last time I encountered the old grave digger before he retired we had taken shelter under a canopy, waiting for the rain to abate so that we might finish our duties and depart. He looked at me wistfully and asked: "Preacher, do you still believe what you say over the dead?" I replied, "I certainly do, otherwise I would not say it."

"Do you believe like this all of the time?" he asked.

I answered, "The circumstances of life drive me occasionally to despair and doubt. But like one who finds the sunlight more brilliant because he has looked at darkness for a season I turn again to the light of faith."

The old man put his calloused hands on my shoulders and said softly, "That's a good way to be, a good way. Especially when you're like me, with so little time to go."

A HOPE TO LIVE BY

Chester A. Pennington

*Professor of Preaching and Worship, Iliff School of Theology
Denver, Colo.*

"Everybody must die his own death." That's the way a thought-ful Christian once put it.

There is evidence that we try to avoid this truth, by refusing to think about it, by distracting ourselves with all kinds of activities. But there is also evidence that we don't get away with such dodges. If we want to live well, we must come to terms with the reality of our own death. And our Christian faith certainly offers us resources for such achievement.

Above all we must face quite honestly the reality of death. It's easy to be sentimental at this point, to pretend that death isn't really real, that we all have an immortal soul which God will take care of somehow, sometime.

We don't have to be Christians to be honest. In fact, some of our contemporaries who are unclear about their faith have achieved a strong attitude towards death.

Stewart Alsop's *Stay of Execution* is an informal account of the way in which the author came to terms with his own impending death. Told that he had leukemia, Stewart Alsop was forced to face the fact that he had only a limited time to live. And he tells an impressive story of courage and good spirit.

Alsop is a confessed agnostic. He simply doesn't know whether there is a God. But he preserves a quaint leftover of childish faith. He sometimes prays to God, Mother, Father, and Aggie (a former nurse). We can hardly believe that the author really takes the prayer seriously. He has no operative faith in God or the possibil-ity of life after death. Yet he comes to a quiet, impressive accept-ance of his impending death, and a genuine gratitude for life. He has not resolved the mystery of suffering, in fact he is still offended by it. But he has learned to live with reality.

We Christians can learn from such honesty. We can reject sentimental refusal to face the facts, we can accept death as real. That is, death may be not just the end of our bodily life, but the end of our very being.

This seems to be the scriptural understanding. Admittedly, there are differences among biblical scholars. But there is wide agreement that the Hebrew understanding of death, which of course is what Jesus began with, was much more serious than the Greek, which is what many of us have been influenced by. In Scripture death means not just the end of the body, but the end of the whole person. By the time Jesus began his ministry, the Jews were debating whether God might raise faithful persons to new life. Jesus seems to have sided with those who affirmed the possibility of resurrection. But this didn't mean an immortal soul automatically surviving the death of the body. This meant God exercising his power to raise persons from death into life.

If this is what Jesus believed, it is what actually happened to Jesus that became the basis for Christian faith.

The Christian faith really took shape after the resurrection of Christ. This was a shattering event which overwhelmed the disciples, which they didn't comprehend, and which they really couldn't believe at first. But finally they were persuaded that God had really raised Christ from the dead. And this faith became the basis for their, and our, hope that followers of Christ might also be raised to eternal life.

The story of the first Easter, if you read the gospels carefully, is a story of fear and unbelief yielding only gradually to hope and faith. The disciples were not superstitious people grasping at any figment of their imagination. They finally believed that God had raised Christ from the dead, only after the evidence became irresistible.

Then they went out telling the story, sharing their faith. We can believe in resurrection, they said, because God has raised Christ from the dead. This is God's triumphant act, destroying the power of death, giving us the asurance of eternal life with him. In the whole fact of Jesus Christ, God has affirmed his power to give and guarantee genuine life.

Easter, then, is not so much a springtime festival as it is the Christian feast of Passover. It was the Passover that Jesus and his disciples celebrated in the Last Supper. That's why Easter comes at the irregular time it does, because it is related to the Passover. This is the Jews' celebration of their liberation from slavery in Egypt. God had delivered them from bondage and realeased them into life as a people.

Easter is the Christian celebration of our liberation from the threat of spiritual death. We are released to live lives of freedom and trust and hope. Physical death need have no real threat for us. It is a necessary and important part of the life process. But it need no longer threaten us with annihilation, with nonbeing, with separation from God, the source of life. Because God, in Christ, has conquered spiritual death, has affirmed his power to give life to his creatures. If we commit ourselves to his purposes and his care, he will raise us up to eternal life.

There are two dimensions to this glad hope: future and present. Both are powerful and important.

The future dimension of the promise is that God will raise us up to a new life in his eternal kingdom. We can become overly curious about the nature of this life. Such curiosity does not really pay, because not much real evidence has been given us. A figure of speech which Paul uses in 1 Corinthians 15 is beautifully appropriate.

God will raise us up to the new life of eternity, Paul writes, and he will give us new bodies which will be adequate to the opportunities of this new life. If you ask me what I mean, he continues, I can only use an analogy.

When you plant a seed or root in the ground, what comes from it is something quite different from the seed or root itself. So that, by looking at a kernel of corn, you could never imagine what a stalk, with ears and tassels, would look like. Or the flowers that grace our homes, churches, and parks—consider what we plant in the ground, a seed or a dried-up-looking root or bulb. And look at the beauty which bursts forth!

This is what we will be given for our life in eternity, says Paul: a new body, quite unlike anything we can imagine, but entirely adequate to the new quality of life in God's eternal kingdom.

Our Christian hope, however, is not just future but also present. Again it is an insight of Paul which is helpful. He mentions in his letters that the power of the resurrection is a power which God offers us for our present use. That is, there are death-dealing powers which can spoil and destroy life. It is not just the threat of death which must be overcome, but also the threat of such deadly attitudes as fear, hostility, anxiety, alienation, lust for power and prestige.

God can deliver us from these destructive attitudes and feelings. The same life-affirming power by which God rasied Christ from the dead can be our present experience, raising us out of self-destroying ways of thinking and living. One place where Paul says this most clearly is Romans 8.11: "If the Spirit of him who raised Jesus from the dead dwells in you, he who raised Christ Jesus from the dead will give life to your mortal bodies also through his Spirit which dwells in you."

You can live gladly and hopefully, right now. Your life can be enriched by the assurance of an eternal life of service and growth in God's eternal kingdom. Your life can be made more gracious and effective by the present power of God in you, healing and enabling you to grow in the attitudes and ways of life that make for wholeness and fulfillment.

There is a beautiful prayer for a deceased person in the Prayer Book of the Episcopal Church. I believe it can apply to us living followers of Christ as well.

"That he (we) may go on from strength to strength, in the life of perfect service, in Thine eternal kingdom."

This may be our hope, not only for the future perfect, but for the present imperfect: That we may go on from strength to strength growing constantly in our capacity to live well and effectively, because of the inner working of the life-giving power of God. This present experience is enhanced and enriched by the hope that in eternity we may still go on from strength to strength, in a life of perfect service, in a new dimension, to which we will be raised by the same life-giving power of God.

THE LAST ENEMY DEFEATED

Michael Rogness

*Pastor, First Lutheran Church
Duluth, Minn.*

Lest anybody have any questions about the sweeping extent of Jesus Christ's triumphant victory over death, let him or her read from the fifteenth chapter of Paul's first Letter to Corinth:

> . . . then shall come to pass the saying that is written:
> "Death is swallowed up in victory.
> "O death, where is thy victory?
> "O death, where is thy sting?"
> . . . thanks be to God, who gives us the victory through our Lord Jesus Christ.

Add to that verse 26: "The last enemy to be defeated is death."

Has it ever occurred to you how on Easter Day, the central day of the church calendar, we invariably come back to the themes of life and death? During the other fifty-one Sundays of the year we deal with all kinds of other themes—joy and sadness, guilt and forgiveness, peace and disturbance, alienation and brotherhood, rejection and acceptance, and a host of others. The Christian faith touches them all. But on Easter Sunday we return to the very central issue of human life, and that is life itself, and death itself.

It is as if on this special Sunday we clear away all these other themes for the time being, as if we peel away all the layers of the onion, and we come right down to the heart of the matter, the central core—life and death.

Ever since the dawn of mankind, the last enemy has been death. No matter what kind of problems man faces, no matter what the circumstances were, or what century it was, man has fought against death, struggling for life.

How has man dealt with death throughout his history? In a number of ways. In the first place, there have been those wealthy enough or resourceful enough who have attempted to beat death. Look at the Pharaohs of ancient Egypt, for instance. They built their great piles of rock we call the pyramids and arranged to have themselves embalmed with mysterious substances so that as mummies their bodies would last through the ages—as if by hiding these preserved bodies in a subterranean pyramid vault death would be outwitted! Of course it did not work. The mighty Pharaohs ended up just as dead as their poorest subjects who were buried in the sand.

And so it goes with all the vain conquerors and exalted people of the world who have tried in one way or another to defeat death by preserving themselves. The English Romantic poet Shelley wrote a sonnet about a monumental statue which lay crumbled in the sands of Africa. It told about a great king, Ozymandias, and you perhaps remember the poem from your high school or college literature classes.

> My name is Ozymandias, king of kings,
> Look on my works, ye Mighty, and despair!
> Nothing beside remains. Round the decay
> Of that colossal wreck, boundless and bare
> The lone and level sands stretch far away . . .

We have our modern equivalents of this urge to preserve oneself. One version, for example, we call "cryonics," the procedure of freezing a body at the point of death, holding it in the deep-freeze until a cure for that particular disease is found, then thawing our subject out, curing the malady, and sending him merrily on his way for another few years of living! I have no idea how many bodies are currently in the freezer, but I suspect both you and I are correct in predicting that they are all as irrevocably dead as their great-grandfathers.

There is another way we have of dealing with death, and this is very popular in our country today: We avoid it. We repress it. It seems to be "the American way" nowadays. We are in love with youth, and we have a haunting fear of growing and looking old.

We even avoid the word "death," preferring to say "pass away" or "expire" instead of just plain "die." When we learn that somebody we know or love is terminally ill in the hospital, we find it awkward to visit that person (and as a matter of pure fact, terminally ill patients do receive fewer visits—just when they need them the most!). Our cheery sickroom bedside manner—"How nice you're getting better!"—collapses when we learn that the sick person is not going to get better, but is about to die.

The wonders of our modern science have insulated us somewhat from death and have made it easier to avoid. In past centuries parents would have six or eight children in the hope that maybe three or four would survive into adulthood. Burying their children was not unusual. Today we have three children in the full expectation that all three will survive us into old age, and it is a wrenching trauma when we lose a child.

Thanks to science we seldom minister to an ailing grandparent slowly dying in the upstairs bedroom. Rather we pay him an occasional visit to the hospital room, where he is hooked up with all sorts of tubes running in and out, and his grandchildren under fourteen are not permitted to see him at all.

If we want to perpetuate the grand illusion of avoiding death, we can even get our faces "lifted," take away those tell-tale wrinkles, which betray advancing age! Yes, we Americans prefer to avoid death. But it always catches us in the end!

The most universal way mankind confronts death is simply to struggle for life and finally to lose. Sooner or later—with good fortune later—your heart and mine will lurch its final beat and lie still, and each one of us will die. There are even those tragic few for whom life is so hopeless and burdensome that they welcome death as escape and oblivion.

This last enemy gets us all, as Thomas Gray reminds us in his "Elegy Written in a Country Churchyard":

> The boast of heraldry, the pomp of power,
>   And all that beauty, all that wealth e'er gave
> Awaits alike the inevitable hour;
>   The paths of glory lead but to the grave.

We have come here today to hear that the fortress citadel of this last enemy has been stormed and taken. Death is defeated. In triumph Paul hurls his almost mocking cry of triumph:

> Now death, where is your victory?
> Now death, where is your sting?

How? How can we defeat death? How does the resurrection of Jesus of Nazareth become our triumph over this last enemy?

The answer begins, curiously enough, *by dying!*

It might sound foolish, but the first step to defeat death is to die. That is what God did: he died! He died in his son Jesus. That sounds even more foolish, as Paul says in 1 Corinthians, but that is what happened. God's son, you might have thought, would defeat death by proving himself invincible, by steamrolling his way through this earthly life impervious to sicknesses, to pain and finally to death, rising back up triumphantly into heaven.

But he did not. He did not deny death, or repress death, or avoid death, as we attempt to do. He died. He embraced death and succumbed. He went through what each one of us will go through, although his gruesome death as an executed criminal was worse than ours will be.

But there is more to the story, and it is this "more" that brings us to worship Sunday after Sunday: He died, yes, but he rose from the dead. And there is the power and the mystery—the secret which unlocks the wonderful song of the Christian gospel.

It just would not have worked had he avoided or escaped death —he would not have been one of us. But since we must die, he too died. Life comes not by avoiding or escaping death, *but by dying!*

There are two dimensions to this astounding gospel:

The first is that we die and will live on beyond our death. There is more to our life than the brief span of time bounded by the years our heart is beating. Jesus rose and lived beyond Good Friday, so that we too might share in his eternal life.

As if that is not astonishing enough, the second aspect to this gospel really takes our breath away: When we accept the crucified and risen Jesus Christ as our Lord, we have died already! We have died already in him, and we are already raised to life eternal in him!

Often as you have heard this, stop now and let it sink in!

In Christ we have died. We were drowned in the water of our baptism. As Luther says in his *Small Catechism*, being baptized in

Christ means that every day the old Adam in us should be drowned, and every day we rise up in Christ's new life.

This is indeed a tremendous gospel! You and I can say, "Yes, I shall die. I do not want to, but I shall die someday. But because I already share in Christ's death through faith, I already live in his resurrection and eternal life."

One of the contemporary musicians in our church today, John Ylvisaker, whom many of you have heard I'm sure, has written a song which pulsates with strength precisely because the powers of the world are powerless to destroy us. Its refrain addresses death and the threats which arise around us:

> You can't kill me; I've already died!
> You've lost your power, my fate to decide!

Is it any wonder that throughout the centuries men and women have drawn courage from the gospel of Jesus Christ? Is it not exhilarating to know that though we have yet to die physically, in Christ we have already died to the power of death and in him are living in his eternal life? The last enemy is defeated, ". . . thanks be to God, who gives us the victory through our Lord Jesus Christ!"

CHRIST IS RISEN!

Alexander Schmemann

Dean and Professor of Liturgical and Pastoral Theology
St. Vladimir's Orthodox Theological Seminary
Crestwood, N.Y.

Every time we see death face to face—the death of someone whom we knew and loved, who was a part of our own life; every time we contemplate this strange immobility, this frightening presence of an absence; every time death reveals to us its inescapable, brutal power over life: all human words seem to lose their significance. Explanations no longer explain; theories and ideas no longer help.

But when death brings to naught all the beautiful theories which seem so meaningful and comforting as long as death itself is but an idea and an abstraction, a distant horizon, maybe it is only then that we can accept again, comprehend again that which we usually forget yet which stands at the very heart of our faith: Christ's own horror of death!

We are so accustomed to the idea that religion's main task and function is to explain and to comfort, to make death into something "normal" and "rational" and thus acceptable, to reconcile us with death, that we forget Christ's attitude toward death. It comes to us as a shock to realize that Christ—when his hour to die approached—began to be "sore amazed and very heavy"; that at the grave of his friend Lazarus, Jesus wept; that nowhere in the gospel can we discover that attitude toward death which seems to have permeated all religions—perhaps even to have produced them and justified them in the eyes of men: the understanding of death as something inescapable and therefore normal, natural and therefore good! No, we are not followers of Plato and of his innumerable disciples who tried—for centuries—to convince men that death is a liberation and must be sought and loved! No, we are not with those who at this horrible hour would quietly and self-confidently dissert about the immortal soul and the "other world"—spiritual and eternal—as taking care of our grief, anxiety and despair.

At this ultimate hour, facing this death, contemplating this face, this unique human being to whom life was given as a divine gift, for whom the whole world was created as his life, his joy, his meaning, we know—with a knowledge that no idea and no theory can destroy—that death is absurd and criminal, a separation that nothing can justify, a destruction with which nothing can reconcile us.

But then all we can do is to follow Christ as he slowly proceeds toward the grave in which his friend Lazarus is hidden from the eyes of man, toward that darkness which once more has swallowed and destroyed the light of life. He sees Mary and Martha, the sisters of Lazarus, weeping "and the Jews also weeping which came with her . . ." And seeing that grief and that despair, he "groaned in the spirit," says the gospel, "and was troubled." He is with us, weeping with us, groaning with us. "Where have you laid him?" he asks. And as they answer unto him "Lord come and see . . ." he himself begins to weep.

It is into the ineffable mystery of those tears that we have to enter. "Lord, come and see. . . ." But what does he see? He sees his friend, the one whom he himself has brought into his marvellous light of life, to whom he himself gave the ineffable beauty of the divine image, for whom he himself has created this world and made it to be very good, he sees this friend taken away, hidden under a stone, separated from life and light, from love and communion, disposed of as refuse for "he stinks . . ."

And seeing this he weeps at the defeat of God by something God has not created: death, at the insult, at the horrible challenge, at the demonic rebellion against life. It is life crying over the destruction of life; it is God contemplating the annihilation of his work.

And what these tears reveal to us then is that we should not accept death or be reconciled with it. For to accept it and to be reconciled with it means that we accept the victory of the enemy, that God has failed in his creation, and that death which he has not cre-

ated is truly the ultimate law of the universe, and the ultimate no
to God.

Thus, it is at the grave of Lazarus that the hour of which Christ
has spoken as *his hour* begins: the hour for which he came; the
hour of the ultimate fight so that the last enemy—death—may be
destroyed.

It is at the grave of Lazarus that he himself makes his entrance
into death. He calls Lazarus back to life—but Lazarus will die
again. This is then just a sign, an announcement, a declaration of
war. No, he himself, in whom is life and who is life, will descend
into dying and death, will partake of all human despair and horror
of death, will taste of its horrible reality. And by doing this, by
accepting this, by assuming death, he will destroy it from inside.
He will trample down death by death.

For his death is only love, only obedience, only compassion. No
one takes his life, but he himself lays it down and thus death itself
is filled with life; death itself becomes the ultimate act and victory
of life.

"Death is swollen by victory!" We offer at this time no comfort
and no help. We only confess and proclaim that in one man death
was overcome, in one man the divine creation was restored, the
ultimate victory won.

Do we believe in him? Do we love him? Do we follow him? If
we do then to this grave, to this man whom death has taken from
us, to this grief and suffering, we have nothing else to say but:
Christ Is Risen!

And his resurrection is ours. It is the mysterious light shining in
the midst of this mortal world. He has entered the dark kingdom
of death; he has filled all things with himself. And thus, even
when we descend into that darkness, we find Christ there, the risen
Lord, the life and the way. And while we still weep, deep down in
our hearts the mysterious joy begins to dawn. A voice says to us:
"Why do you cry?" A certitude comes that death has been overcome and its dominion has been shaken.

Christ is risen!

AGENTS OF LIFE IN A DYING WORLD

Herman G. Stuempfle, Jr.

*Dean, Lutheran Theological Seminary
Gettysburg, Pa.*

This text of Luke 7:11–16 drops us without warning right into the middle of a battle. It's a battle in a war that's been raging since the beginning of time. You could write the whole history of man in terms of it. It's the story of each of our lives. It's the conflict between life and death.

In this gospel story, the battle is joined between Jesus, the lord of life, and a young man who's a recent victim of death. But Jesus and the widow's son aren't solitary combatants. Each has an army behind him. Luke tells us, ". . . his disciples and a great crowd went with [Jesus]" toward the city of Nain. At precisely the same moment, "there was a large crowd" in a funeral procession winding out of the city. Viewed from a reconnaisance plane, they would have looked exactly like the columns of two opposing armies advancing toward each other without either knowing. Suddenly and unexpectedly they meet at the city gate: the army of life, with Jesus at its head; the army of death, with a dead boy and his sobbing mother at its head. Which will go away victorious?

Of course, we know the answer to that question, because we know the ending of this story; and we'll return to that later. Right now I want to raise a more personal question. In which army are you marching? I have a conviction that each of us does march in one or the other and that it's a matter literally of life and death importance which one it is.

Let's look first at the army of death. It isn't just that little band moving through Nain long ago. They only acted out on a small scale the death march of the entire human race. You can see it in history taken as a whole. Arnold Toynbee has counted up more

than twenty civilizations which have lived for an instant in glory
and then died. Egypt, Babylon, Assyria, Greece, Rome—all great
living cultures now in their graves. And the march goes on. In our
time, we've seen Nazi Germany, the "master race," lift itself to the
skies, only to be buried in the ashes of self-destruction. Likewise,
we saw the splendor of Imperial Japan, the "Empire of the Rising
Sun"; and we watched the sun go down.

It leads us to ask, "What about us? When will the bell toll for
us?" What has been the meaning of slaughter and defoliation in
Southeast Asia, of violence in our cities, of hunger in our pockets
of poverty, of poison in our streams and air, of corruption in the
highest places, of the population bomb quietly ticking away? Are
these the death rattle of still another great civilization—this time
our own?

You can also hear the tramp of death in our individual lives.
Usually we manage to drown the sound beneath the noise of our
frantic schedules. But now and then something happens which
almost slaps us in the face with the realization that we're born to
die. It may be a close call on the freeway, a stab of fear when our
plane comes in to land, a sickness that carries us right to the brink,
the death of somebody close to us. We call birth the beginning of
life and rejoice when a new child is born into the world. Might it
not be just as realistic to call it the beginning of death—and weep?

We should note, however, that when Jesus, the lord of life,
speaks about death, he doesn't always mean this inevitable end
toward which each of us is moving. He speaks of death in another
way. Listen! "I tell you, my friends, do not fear those who kill the
body and after that have no more that they can do. But I will warn
you whom to fear: fear him who, after he has killed has power to
cast into hell." (Luke 12:4, 5)

There's a death that can precede the death of the body, and is
more deadly still. This death kills life at its center. It doesn't stop
the heart; it destroys the self. It's the death that strangles faith,
crushes hope, poisons love, smothers prayer. I think for most of us
it's a creeping death, overcoming us so slowly and subtley that
we're hardly aware it's happening. Our good life isolates us from
the victims of our society, and we gradually lose our capacity to
care. Our drive to get ahead pushes us into a compromise here and

a short cut there, and the voice of conscience begins to fade. We get busy with a thousand things, most of them good things, but the one thing—the thing without which we can't live, the hidden line of life between ourselves and God—shrivels from neglect. Pray that when we reach such boundaries of death, we'll hear the warning shout of the lord of life: "For what does it profit a man to gain the whole world and forfeit his soul? For what can a man give in exchange for his soul?" (Mark 8:36, 37) What use is it to march—if it's in the army of death?

And we do march there, all of us; and there'd be no hope for us if it weren't for another, opposing force, always swiftly, silently on the move, which again and again intercepts us at the gate. Today, in Luke's story, that force confronts us in the person of Jesus. As the dead boy and the widowed mother move slowly with their retinue of weeping friends on the death march to the cemetery outside the city gates, this other army—all unknown to them —is marching toward the city. They might have passed without an engagement, except for one thing. Jesus takes in the situation at a glance. He sees the dead boy and the weeping mother, and no husband to comfort her. "Do not weep," he calls. Swiftly he moves to lay his hand on the bier. The pallbearers stop. The lord of life speaks to the victim of death: "Young man, I say to you, arise!" "And the dead man," Luke tells us, "sat up."

I can't tell you exactly what happened in that instant, or how it happened. Too much time has elapsed since that particular battle, and battle reports from distant wars are notoriously hard to transcribe into exact records. But that isn't important. What is important is to tell you that this lord of life is on the field *now*—at this moment, in this world of death, in these dying lives of ours—with power to give us life.

During the war in Southeast Asia, I read a news release about a widow in Detroit who on a Thursday received word that her son had been killed in Vietnam. Friday morning, official confirmation of his death arrived from the Defense Department. Then, Friday afternoon, a telegram came saying it had all been a mistake. Her son was alive! They were flying him home to her on special leave. It was Nain in Detroit! Life out of death! Or so it must have seemed to that mother.

And the word of the gospel is that it's Nain where *you* live. The Lord who has power to bring life out of death stands by your side and says, "Arise!"

He says that to each of us whom fear or guilt or despair or loneliness is always trying to kill inside before it's time for us to die; and he tells us that he never abandons us to these or any other agents of death. Any word that faith or hope or love is dead in your life is always premature—even when you say it to yourself. Likewise, he comes to us who are always only a heart-beat away from the grave, either our own or of those we love; and he tells us we needn't fear *that* kind of death, either. He walked himself through the dark "valley of the shadow" and came out on the other side to be God's "rod and staff" to comfort us when we must make the same journey. He comes to us also in our anxiousness for the fate of our world, careening along on what often looks like a suicidal path. He bears God's faithful promise that even when we persist in laying waste his creation and turning history into a bloodbath, he's ceaselessly at work toward that day in which there shall be "a new heaven and a new earth in which righteousness dwell."

When you receive this promise and power of life, when in the midst of death you find yourself marching in the army of life, then you'll become in your turn an agent of life to the world. Has it ever struck you as strange that the writers of the Gospels seldom report the sequels to the miracles they relate? They rarely tell us what became of those persons to whom Jesus in some way gave new life. Blind Bartimaeus, for example: did he use his new sight only to look out for himself—or to search out other men's needs, as Jesus had searched out his? The man with the crippled arm: did he use his new strength to beat on the weak and grab from the poor—or to lift burdens from men's backs as Jesus had lifted a burden from his? Or, this widow's son: did he use his new life only to descend into the more terrible death of a life centered on himself, thus becoming an agent of death in a world already dying for lack of love—or, in his new life, did he become an extension of the love of that one who had given him life?

Few sequels, I say, are writtten to these miracle stories of the Gospels, but every day we write the sequel to ours. We write it either in terms of our indifference to dying men in a dying world, or, in terms of reaching out, where we are, to bring, in the words of St. Francis, "where there is doubt, faith; where there is despair, hope; where there is darkness, light; where there is sadness, joy."

No one else can say what that will mean for you concretely. The actions of life in a world of death are infinitely varied. They can range all the way from writing a long neglected letter to holding out persistent friendship to a neighbor who abuses it to plunging into the struggle for a more just and human society. Often the actions of life will cost something. But that shouldn't come as a surprise, for life reached us by way of a man dying on a cross.

A number of years ago I knew a widow whose only son, though not dead, was confined to an institution for epileptics. He was also mentally retarded. He could neither read nor write. However, a regular correspondence flowed between mother and son, because an older man, himself a prisoner of epilepsy, took it upon himself to read and write letters for this boy who could do neither. One day the mother showed me a letter she'd just received from her faithful correspondent. At the bottom of the page he'd written a quotation which had obviously become a force in his own afflicted life: "May the love of God, which is our life, teach us the love of man, which is our task."

He was marching in the right army.

Are you?

GRIEF: PERSONAL AND COMMON

William R. Snyder

Pastor, St. John's Lutheran Church
Minneapolis, Minn.

In the early morning hours of July 28th, I heard a very familiar voice on the phone utter these very strange and shocking words: "You have just lost your mother." It was my father's voice telling me that mother had died suddenly just after her sixty-fourth birthday.

During my grief experience, a St. John's member asked me how I found being the bereaved instead of being the one who ministered to the bereaved. As I turned this question over it seemed to me it may be good for me to say some things this morning about my grief experience in the hope of being helpful to others. For while grief is very personal, it is also very common.

First, I felt and continued to feel for several days a flood of negative emotions rolling in over me like a mighty, irresistible tidal wave: the same negative emotions we see in the lives of the Lord's followers when they lost Jesus through his death on the cross. Mary Magdalene and the other women rushing to the grave in the garden on the first Easter morn experienced the gnawing emotion of loneliness. They missed the Master's peaceful, powerful presence.

The two disciples on the road to Emmaus were filled with frustration. They told the unknown stranger (who was the resurrected Christ) who joined them along the dusty road, that they had hoped that Jesus was the long awaited Messiah. But their great hope had been smashed to smithereens by the soldier's hammer nailing Jesus to the cross. Judas and Peter were filled with guilt. Peter's guilt immobilized him and so he did not accompany the women to the garden grave. The guilt of Judas drove him to suicide.

77

We see anger in Thomas. His words not only express doubt but also reveal anger. He seems to be angry with Jesus for having disappointed him. Thomas' disappointment will be overcome only if Jesus meets his precise demands—demands forged by the fires of anger. We see fear in all the followers of Jesus and so they run and hide in the upper room.

I experienced all of these negative emotions. I felt quite frustrated because I had come within several days of seeing my mother again. My frustration was great since I had initially planned my vacation in July and then switched to August because of the program at Chi Rho, our camp and retreat center. Anger also filled my heart—anger with the doctor for what I felt was his somewhat lackadaisical treatment of mother; anger with God—it seemed to me he could have preserved her life another five days—even anger with mother for neglecting to conserve her failing energy by following a more moderate schedule.

Guilt also tugged at my heart: guilt for the many letters I did not write—some church business always seemed more important—guilt for not having come sooner. Fear also blew across my heart like an intermittent icy wind out of the arctic, especially fear for my father who would now be all alone. Loneliness lashed at me—how empty my parents' home seemed to be without mother. My son, David, expressed this emptiness when he said, "Grandma always made me feel so welcome, so good, she made me feel she loved me and now she's gone." It seems to me losing one's mother, the one in whom one's very being was fashioned, brings a special kind of loneliness.

Yes, I experienced all of the negative emotions the disciples experienced when they lost Jesus through death: emotions common to all human beings when they walk through the valley of the shadow of death over the loss of a loved one. It helped me to know that these negative emotions are very normal—very human. Thus I did not try to gloss them over—to tell myself that they did not exist. Instead of trying to hide from the truth of their existence, I could honestly face them, which is the first step towards overcoming them. It also helped to know that God forgives such negative emotions and that my mother would understand. Such wonderful knowledge made it possible for me to forgive myself.

Second, my grief experience taught me the great importance of honestly recognizing that life with mother was in fact over as far as life on this earth is concerned. It was comforting to reminisce, to recall joyous occasions, to talk for hours about the periods of happiness we had together. It was especially pleasing to me when I could travel way back on the dusty road of memory and recount some thrilling moment with Mom that Dad had forgotten.

It was comforting to think how I tried so hard to please her and to remember the genuine joy she derived from my ministry. It was comforting to think of how tenderly her life touched our lives and of the many things she did for us. It was also comforting to contemplate the many things she did for others. The fact that most of her pallbearers were under thirty was comforting to me personally, because it was a testimony to her unending interest in young people and in other people's children.

Yes, marvelous memories of mother's life brought real comfort but her life on this earth had ended. My youngest child gave beautiful expression to this truth when our family stood with tearfilled eyes by mother's casket; she said: "Don't cry daddy, we'll just have to have all our fun with Grandpa from now on." I thought of the words of Scripture: "And a little child shall lead them."

The natural thing is to want to hang on, to cling to the memories, to relive the past—and this is good—but it is not good when it is indulged in to the point that we refuse to come to grips with the fact that our loved one is dead as far as life on this earth is concerned. We should no longer foolishly attempt to invest anything of ourselves in our departed loved one.

Instead we should now invest ourselves in the living—we should now invest our energies in others. We must now carve out a new life that does not include our departed loved one. To do so, to go on living creatively and triumphantly is to truly honor our departed loved one. That's what my little girl was saying when she remarked: "We will just have to have all our fun with Grandpa from now on."

Third, my experience underscored the foolishness of mourning alone. When we lose a loved one through death, the temptation is exceedingly great to go off by ourselves and bear our grief alone. Isolation is truly insidious and causes mental illness. We need

other people in order to keep in touch with reality, in order to
help us bear our grief, in order to stay healthy.

Being surrounded by the congregation at the funeral service was
very helpful. I had the feeling that the congregation, made up of
loved ones, were there to support, strengthen, and sustain. And I
felt this strength, support, and sustenance emanating from them.
The inspiring messages that I received from so many of you I
found truly helpful even though you were a thousand miles away.
Yes, to mourn alone is to invite misery from which one may not
recover. We need other people.

Perhaps I should add here that we ought to mourn. There are
still some people who wrongly believe that to mourn is a sign of
shallow faith or no faith at all: while to show no external signs of
mourning is the manifestation of a firm faith. Some people still
wrongly believe that crying is a sign of weakness. They forget that
Jesus wept. Unhappily all too many children in the past have been
taught that the shedding of tears is a sign of not being grown-up.
When mother died—except for the brief time during which the
service was held for her—the heavens wept for eight days. In light
of her good life, the weeping of the heavens seemed appropriate to
me. I wept too.

Tears are God's gift. They are a safety valve God has given us
to release great inner emotional pressure. If we refuse to mourn, if
we hold back the tears, the inner emotional pressure will build up
to an explosive state. This is exceedingly dangerous. We must ever
remember Christ once said, "Blessed are those who mourn—for
they shall be comforted." Only when we mourn can Christ fill us
with his comfort.

Finally, in my grief experience what meant more to me than
anything else was my faith in Jesus Christ and the hope of eternal
life which he gives to us. I rejoiced in the fact that this was far
beyond a matter of the mind—far beyond giving one's intellectual
assent to a body of theological ideas. Instead it was the marvelous
faith Jesus talked to Peter about at Caesarea-Phillippi—the faith
that is a gift from God and not man-generated. This God-given
faith fills one with assurance and one truly feels the meaning of the
old gospel hymn, "Blessed Assurance."

In my grief I discovered that something I had told others for years is true: when one loses a loved one through death the hardest thing is to accept the reality of the loved one's death. Now with our minds we can readily accept the fact of a loved one's death, but accepting with one's entire being is another matter. After all, we have oriented our life—our whole being—around the life of our departed loved one. We have invested so much of our entire being in his or her being.

Thus for our entire being to make the adjustment is exceedingly difficult. Our life must be reorientated; our feelings and emotions must be healed. Here is where I found a God-given faith so very helpful. The Great Physician began healing my wounded emotions; he began soothing my bruised feelings. The spirit of Christ helped me reorient my life.

I discovered that human reason is truly helpless in the face of death. We overcome death with God-given faith, a faith that fills us with blessed assurance—the blessed assurance that our loved one is not dead but living still. For me, the high point of the entire experience was the funeral service in the church. Through the singing of the hymns, the reading of the Scripture, and the pastor's proclamation of the gospel I felt the spirit of Christ coming: surrounding me and permeating my being. His spirit filled me with the assurance that mother was not dead but living still.

Thus I went with Christian confidence to the cemetery. I was pleased with the beautiful Pennsylvania hillside in which her body was placed. But I did not feel that she was in that grave. Instead I felt that she was with us and she shared in the fellowship of family and friends. I continue to feel that she is with me. It was always a great thrill for her to hear me preach but she rarely had the opportunity to do so. Now I feel that she can be present for every worship service here at St. John's. I rejoice in this knowledge and give thanks to Jesus Christ for this blessed assurance.

THE STING OF DEATH

Paul A. Washburn

*Bishop, Chicago Conference, United Methodist Church
Chicago, Ill.*

How presumptuous it is to preach about death. We know nothing about it from personal experience for we have not experienced it ourselves. We may conjecture about death if we have watched carefully while someone else died. As a pastor I have watched many persons die. Death has a sting to it. As a son and a father I have watched my parents and my son-in-law die. Death has a sting to it. St. Paul lifted a good question.

O Death, where is thy sting?

I

One of the stings of death is that it separates the dying one from enjoyment of the created world.

In life our sense mechanisms of seeing, hearing, tasting, smelling, touching give us access to the creation; not to the whole of it at any one time, for it is too vast; not to the intensity of it in any one place, for it is very dense; and not to the potential of it in any one experience, for it is always growing and changing. But we can see a sunset or a star in a night-time sky. We can hear a bird's song or a symphony. We can taste an apple or spinach. We can smell the aroma of burning leaves or freshly baked bread. We can touch one another. We are sensuous beings when we are truly alive. That is, we can, by using our sense mechanisms, experience our environment.

But it is surely true that we are always parting company with the environment we are sensing.

Once my father dug a tunnel for me through a bank of snow.

He enjoyed the digging of it. I enjoyed running through it. Soon spring came and the snow melted. The memory of the tunnel lingers for five and a half decades. The real thing is gone, I can remember it but I can't touch it or feel its coldness. It is gone. I am parted from it. That's like the sting of death.

Once a pastor of one of our churches in the German Democratic Republic guided me through the Swinger, that exquisite museum of art in Dresden. Three sensations of that trip remain: the sight of numerous Russian soldiers in the museum, the Sixtische Madonna, and the ruin of the Castle of the Saxon Kings just outside the window. I took all that and more in through my senses. Now all that is memory. I doubt that I shall ever sense it again. I am parted from the reality of it. That's like the sting of death.

One summer we visited Yosemite National Park. There were dashing streams and quiet pools. The Park is famous for waterfalls and massive rock formations, El Capitan among them. The formations were, to me, more impressive even than Yosemite Falls. I saw the rocks and the falls with my eyes. I heard the tumbling waters with my ears. I remember Yosemite but probably will not sense it again. The sting of death is like being parted from actually sensing all that beauty and grandeur.

Once almost forty years ago the woman who is now my wife and I sat on a park bench in Evanston, Illinois. A full moon was coming up over Lake Michigan. The grasses beneath our feet were a carpet of green. The air was pungent with the aroma of flowers and we were holding hands . . . touching one another. We still hold hands. I suspect, other things being equal, we'll be holding hands when one of us dies. Then a moment will come when the dying one of us will no longer sense that we are holding hands. Sensorily we will be parted. That's the sting of death.

To be sure I have used affirmative illustrations. Negative illustrations are available also. For our environment, our context, our matrix holds ugliness as well as beauty and much that is neither ugly nor beautiful. Even so, it is a grand experience to sense life and I, for one, do not look forward happily, just now, to being parted forever from it.

One way to soften this sting of death is to sense the environment lavishly without deserting it or outselves. See it! Hear it! Taste it!

Smell it! Touch it! That pulls the stinger of the sting of death at least a bit.

O Death, here is thy sting!

II

Another of the stings of death is that it separates the dying one from enjoyment of that dying one's body.

Our son-in-law Ron had a marvelous body as well as being a specialist in transactional analysis. He was an all-star quarterback in high school. He outplayed footballers one and a half times his size in college. He was an excellent pole-vaulter. He was never over-weight, never intemperate. Even so in mid-1972 cancer was discovered in his body. From the day of the discovery on, over a period of ten months, he had two bouts with surgery and numerous radiation treatments, and then he died.

Ron was a realist about his condition but he also appreciated his body. During his journey into death he went through the stages commonly experienced by the dying. One phase of that journey is especially relevant here. While in Billings Hospital for an extended stay he had a pin-up on his night stand. It was a picture of a vigorous, muscular, healthy male athlete. Ron would say, "In six months I'll look like that again". Alas, it was not to be. Ron was parted from his fine body turned cancerous. That's the sting of death.

Some of us use our bodies as though they were made of the same stuff as El Capitan in Yosemite National Park. Ron didn't do that but death still stung him. Some of the rest of us do spend our bodies recklessly and death will sting us, also. To take care of our bodies as much as possible is one way to at least delay this sting of death for some of us a bit.

O Death! here is thy sting!

III

Yet another of the stings of death is that it separates us from loved ones.

It would have been possible to treat this sting under the first point but that would have treated loves ones as things, not as persons. Loved ones are not things. They are precious persons.

After watching many persons, most of them dearly beloved, die, I have noticed that there comes a moment of resignation when the dying one seems to go off alone. Perhaps it is the moment of realization that earth-bound people can provide no more help. Perhaps it is the moment of realization that those who are to remain earth-bound a bit longer cannot go along. Perhaps it is—for some at least—the moment of realization that one is transfering from near relationship with earth-tied loved ones to near relationship with eternally free loved ones. No matter what characterizes the moment, its reality is separation from the real presence of loved ones. That's part of the sting of death.

It may be possible to make better preparation for this part of the sting of death than it is for the other parts. In the excellent twin films "The Immigrants" and "The New Land" the young wife and mother, Christina, struggles with the problem of being parted from her homeland and especially from her homefolks. Her malady is called homesickness. In it she is depressed. She weeps. She prays. She gets a foretaste of the sting of death. It is lonely. It is painful. It is preparation for the ultimate sting of death.

Five times during my ministerial career I have been reappointed —each time leaving a Christian community of loving and lovable persons. To be sure, they were often troubled and sometimes troublesome. To be sure, they were pilgrim people experiencing meetings and partings also. To be sure, they knew both alienations and reconciliations. And they were beautiful. Each time we left such a community we experienced parting and we had our share of grief work to do. Our relationships were not utterly destroyed but we were deprived of situations in which we could keep the linkages current. Such separations can be preparation for the ultimate sting of death.

O Death, here is thy sting!

This homily on the sting of death is an effort to face realities we can conjecture about death. There are helps in such realism but there are not answers. The best answers are faith-born. And faith causes Christians to look for answers in the everlasting love of the resurrected Christ.

A year ago our United Methodist Council of Bishops heard

Mahler's *Resurrection Symphony* at the John F. Kennedy Center for the Performing Arts. The program notes included the following description of the last movement:

> "The voice of doom is heard. The end of all living things has come. The last judgment is proclaimed and all the terror of the Day of Days breaks forth. The earth trembles, graves spring open, the dead arise and stream forth in an endless procession. The great and the small of this earth, kings and beggars, the just and the unjust— all pass by. Cries for pity and mercy are frightful in our ears. [Death's sting indeed.]
>
> "The scene grows ever more terrifying—all our senses fail us, our consciousness dims at the approach of the Last Judgment. The great summons sounds; the Apocalytic trumpets peal. In the midst of the ghastly stillness we seem to hear a far-away, far-away nightingale, like a last trembling echo of earthly life. [Death's sting indeed!]
>
> "Softly the heavenly and Holy Choir entones: 'Arise, yea, thou shalt arise!' Then appears the splendor of God! A marvelous light suffused us. All is quiet and holy. And see now! There is no judgment, there is no just, no unjust—no great and no small—no punishment and no reward! An over-powering sense of love envelops us with Holy Being and understanding."

There goes the sting of death! It is swallowed up in the splendor of God. It is enveloped in God's scandalous and holy love.

O Death, where is thy sting?